PRESSED DOWN BUT NOT FORGOTTEN

H. Curtis Lyon and John Juern

DEPRESSION

NORTHWESTERN PUBLISHING HOUSE
Milwaukee, Wisconsin

Library of Congress Card 93-84289
Northwestern Publishing House
1250 N. 113th St., Milwaukee, WI 53226-3284
© 1993 by Northwestern Publishing House.
Published 1993
Printed in the United States of America
ISBN 0-8100-0490-9

Contents

While serving as pastor at Trinity Lutheran Church in Crete, Illinois, Curt Lyon has done extensive pastoral counseling. His master's thesis toward the degree of Master of Systematic Theology from Wisconsin Lutheran Seminary in Mequon, Wisconsin, was on *Pastoral Counseling and Psychology*. He is also the author of *Counseling at the Cross*, published by Northwestern Publishing House.

Dr. John Juern is a practicing psychologist, the clinical director of an out-patient mental health clinic, and a professor of psychology at Wisconsin Lutheran College in Milwaukee, Wisconsin. He has served as a Lutheran elementary school teacher, a family counselor at Wisconsin Lutheran Child and Family Service, and now, for more than eight years, a psychologist in private practice.

Editor's Preface

Christians in Crisis Series

At some time in our lives, every one of us faces a crisis. We wonder who we are, what we are doing, what's happening to us, why we face certain problems. Many crises come and go, and we get through them with relative ease. Others flood into our lives and threaten our well-being—lingering, smothering, overwhelming.

This series of books addresses such potentially destructive crises in a Christian's life, and offers God's help to the Christian in crisis. You will learn from these books how God's law and gospel apply to each crisis. You will find how God's Word can help you in your most critical need.

To ensure the integrity and the practical value of this series, each volume has the combined wisdom of a writing team with both theological and scientific training, usually a pastor and a psychologist. All the writers are Christians, who look first to the Scriptures for their guidance.

Northwestern Publishing House offers these little books to you as sources to help you understand and even as tools to help fix what is bothering you. We caution you, however, that they are not meant to offer you an exhaustive treatment to be used in place of personal counseling. Where crisis patterns persist, we urge you to seek counseling from professionals in the field.

Finally, we present this series with the prayer that all your crises may be restored to calm in Christ.

"Come to me, all you who are weary and burdened, and I will give you rest. Take my yoke upon you and learn from me, for I am gentle and humble in heart, and you will find rest for your souls" (Matthew 11:28,29).

Gary P. Baumler

CHAPTER ONE

Christians Suffer Depression Too ~~~

Carol was 43 years old. Her three children were no longer at home. Two were married; one was in college. She had more time on her hands than she knew what to do with. She thought about going to work, but she couldn't seem to summon the necessary energy. She slept late in the morning, watched television most of the day, and very seldom set foot outside the house. Although she was home all day, the house had actually looked better when the children were constantly running through it. To make matters worse, Carol was gaining weight because she snacked constantly and had no energy for exercise. She couldn't remember feeling more miserable.

Carol was a Christian—yet Carol was depressed. Left to herself she probably wouldn't have done anything about her problem, because she simply didn't have the energy to do so. She thought no one could possibly understand what she was going through. In reality, however, some people might have understood.

Depression and God's people

As a committed Christian, you are seeking a solution to the difficult problem of depression, often called the common cold of emotional disorders. Perhaps you or someone you know is feeling depressed. As your fellow Christians, committed to Christ and his Word, we want to enable you both to understand and to deal with depression better.

But understanding depression is only the beginning. We also want you to find hope in the depression you are experiencing. Or, if you are seeking to help someone else who is mired down in depression, we want to enable you to help that person find hope in the midst of his or her depression. To do so, this book will tell you what psychology and psychiatry have to say on the subject, and what solutions they have to offer. That is important. But even more important, this book will lead you to understand depression from God's point of view and give you the answers and solutions God provides in his Word. In addition, it will show you how your study of Scripture and your prayers are an important part of the healing process when you deal with depression.

A definition of depression

A fuller definition and description of depression will follow in successive chapters, but for now, let's begin with a simple definition. To depress means literally *to press down.* Think of something pressing or pushing down on your body and mind, and you will begin to get the picture of what depression is.

Do you feel pressed down? Do you know someone who feels that way? It's a real battle. From time to time, most people have had the feeling of being down. You may even have talked about your "down" days. That's perfectly normal. In depression, however, "down" is more than just a feeling. In depression something is actually pressing down on you, and it makes feeling "up" extremely difficult, if not impossible. A depressed person may find himself engaged in a real battle— fighting to feel "up" again. Conversely, he or she may have already given up the battle because it's proven just too difficult.

Depression, then, is usually more than just an emotional problem. It affects you physically, mentally, and spiritually. Depression can be complicated in the way that it affects you. But for now, just think of depression in terms of its simple definition—being pressed down.

God knows depression is real

Depression is real. Young and old experience it. It causes distress in the lives of Christians and non-Christians. You may feel alone. You may feel hopeless, helpless, sad, lethargic, and even suicidal. Anyone can become depressed. You know that. But when you feel depressed, you may wonder whether God knows it. When depression hits, God often seems far removed, unconcerned, uncaring, even unaware of your suffering.

The cause of depression can be physiological, psychological, or spiritual, or any combination of these. Poor eating and sleeping habits or a lack of exercise can also cause depression, or they might be the result of depression. A serious loss, anger turned inward, or guilt that remains unresolved can all cause depression. When you consider such causes, you can see how important it is to know that God has not removed himself.

God, who knows all things, knows about depression too. He understands how many ways you can be "pressed down" in a world suffering the ravages of sin. It is still true, as Jesus said: "Your Father knows what you need before you ask him" (Matthew 6:8). And God's promise remains forever true: "Never will I leave you; never will I forsake you. So we [can] say with confidence, 'The Lord is my helper; I will not be afraid'" (Hebrews 13:5,6).

He under- stands how many ways you can be "pressed down" in a world suffering the ravages of sin.

9

God knows our needs, even when we experience depression. He is there for us through his Son Jesus. Through the gift of Jesus, our Savior, God deals, as no one else can, with the guilt and anger that can accompany depression. God knows, and God helps.

The value of modern psychology and psychiatry

Modern psychology and psychiatry have done a great deal to enhance our understanding of depression. As a result of their pioneering work, we can recognize depression and define it more specifically. We can identify different types of depression. We can identify different causes of depression.

This information is a tremendous blessing for Christians who, directly or indirectly, experience depression. Whether you are experiencing depression yourself or you are attempting to help someone else who is suffering from depression, much of the information provided by the secular community can be of great value to you. You need to know when you need help, what signs to watch for. You also need to know where you can find the help you need and what kind of help is available. This book, drawing on the information provided by modern psychology and psychiatry, will give you that kind of information.

Another common misconception is that Christians don't get depressed, or, at least, they shouldn't get depressed.

Misconceptions about depression

Many people, including Christians, have misconceptions about depression. Some, for example, think that since their Bibles don't use the words *depression* and *depressed*, God, therefore, has nothing to say about this serious problem. But God does have something to say about it. In fact, Scripture says a great deal about depression. It's just that Scripture does not use the clinical terms from secular psychology or psychiatry. Rather it describes or pictures depression and its effects.

Another common misconception is that Christians don't get depressed, or, at least, they shouldn't get depressed. Some people, like Job's friends, whom he called "miserable comforters" (Job 16:1), will say things like, "You wouldn't have this problem if you had a stronger faith." Saying depression shouldn't happen only serves to make people who already feel guilty and weak feel more guilty and weak. Yes, it happens; Christians suffer from depression.

Still another misconception is that conquering depression is so simple and easy that God didn't consider it necessary to say anything about it. You may hear unsympathetic people say, "If you would just get busy and do something, everything would be okay." That notion is usually bandied about by people who have never experienced depression. But a depressed person cannot change so easily, and God knows that too.

Where these misconceptions lead

Misconceptions about God's concern for depression can lead to serious consequences. These misconceptions can cause people to neglect the most obvious and essential source of help, comfort, and peace God makes available—his Word. The Word of God can and will provide you with the power of Christ who fought sin and Satan and won. At the cost of his own life, Jesus won peace, and he will share that peace with you. When, in the midst of your depression, you've almost forgotten how it feels to be at peace, you need his kind of peace, and he wants you to have it.

Does the following situation sound familiar?

Edward read everything he could find on the subject of depression. But since he thought he had to find the answers to his depression by his own reading and research, he wanted nothing to do with his church or with the Word of God. Edward, however, didn't find the answers and solutions he was looking for. He didn't find them for one simple reason: he had already ruled out God as a source of comfort and relief.

Misconceptions about depression lead people further away from God. Most people, when facing surgery, wouldn't hesitate to look both to a medical doctor and to the Lord for physical and spiritual healing. Still, Satan is able to convince many people that they must face depression on their own, without God. Satan would like us to believe that God doesn't know anything about depression. He would like us to believe that God doesn't understand, that God can't help, that God won't help.

Rather than turning to God for help, the depressed may not feel worthy of God's help. He or she might ask, "Why should God care about a person as pathetic as I am?" When you are depressed, you feel worthless. That is when you need to hear once again that God not only made you, but in love he sent his Son to die for you. He did that for people—people like you. His love was the only reason he did it—his love for you in particular and everyone else as well. Why should God have anything to do with a person like you? The

Why should God have anything to do with a person like you? The answer is grace, pure undeserved love.

answer is grace, pure undeserved love. It's there and at work even when you can't see it clearly from your point of view, even when you are pressed down, feeling down, and looking down at your own situation instead of up at God.

Examples of depression

Do you still doubt whether God knows anything about depression or how well he understands it? Would you like to see? Maybe you'd like to see the kinds of cures God can provide for you. Then take a look at these examples that will show you the way God understands, describes, and gives peace to people who are depressed.

Consider Cain when God confronted him with the murder of his brother, and Cain refused to confess his guilt:

> But on Cain and his offering he did not look with favor. So Cain was very angry, and his face was downcast. Then the Lord said to Cain, "Why are you angry? Why is your face *downcast*?" (Genesis 4:5,6)

Cain's appearance made it evident that something was wrong. He looked sad, troubled, bothered by something that wasn't right. His downcast look gave him away. Cain was depressed. His guilt registered in his face. God recognized his depression. He knew its cause.

Have you ever been able to look at someone and see that something was wrong? Haven't we all had experiences like that? You've probably had someone tell you how you felt when they looked at you. Were you surprised that someone else could see your inner feelings, your depression, so clearly?

What others may see on the surface may go very deep within. The psalmist went behind mere physical appearance when he described his emotions. He addressed his own despondent soul: "Why are you downcast, O my soul? Why so disturbed within me? . . . My soul is downcast within me. . . . Why are you downcast, O my soul? Why so disturbed within me?" (Psalm 42:5,6,11). Similarly in Psalm 43:5 the psalmist writes: "Why are you downcast, O my soul? Why so disturbed within me?" The feeling of being "downcast" strikes at the core of our being. The psalmist's very soul was disturbed in his depression. His troubles lay deep within, where he needed God to reach. And God does reach our innermost being. He cares for us, body and soul. He sent Jesus to save us, both body and soul, for time and for eternity.

God wants more for you than that you feel better and function better. He wants you to *be better.*

In this biblical example, we see an important distinction between secular psychology and psychiatry's approach and God's approach. Secular psychology and psychiatry are not usually concerned about the soul. Secular psychology is happy to be able to help people feel better and function better. The soul isn't part of their usual consideration because one cannot deal with a soul scientifically. But God deals with the soul. God understands the nature of the human being he created, whom he gave both body and soul. God wants more for you than that you feel better and function better. He wants you to be better. You can't ignore your immortal soul and really be better.

In Psalm 32:3,4, David sounds extra depressed. As he recalled his sin of adultery and murder and the associated guilt of his unrepented sin, he wrote, "When I kept silent, my bones wasted away through my groaning all day long. For day and night your hand was heavy upon me; my strength was sapped as in the heat of summer." The weight of his guilt pressed down upon David.

God knows our sinful nature. He understands, too, the blindness sin causes. That blindness to the truth can often accompany depression. Another psalmist asked the question many Christians today ask: "Why do the righteous suffer?" He apparently measured his welfare strictly by earthly standards, forgetting God's eternal plan. "When my heart was grieved and my spirit embittered, I was senseless and ignorant; I was a brute beast before you" (Psalm 73:21,22). In his state of mind, the psalmist could not see that his eternal welfare was far more important than anything else. He was blinded for the time, but God wasn't.

As we consider the ways God shows that he understands and works to heal depression, we must also understand the tools God uses. God always deals with us through his Word. In his Word, God speaks both law and gospel.

One of the clearest examples of God's work through his Word is found in the way Nathan confronted David with his sin. David had committed adultery and murder and suffered depression because of it. He had lived for nearly a year with the guilt his sins caused. Nathan brought David the Word of God, both law and gospel. The law of God spoke directly to David when Nathan said, "You are the man" (2 Samuel 12:7).

David recognized his sin when he saw it reflected in the mirror of God's law. He said, "I have sinned against the Lord" (2 Samuel 12:13).

The gospel brought God's assurance, as Nathan promised, "The Lord has taken away your sin. You are not going to die" (2 Samuel 12:13).

God confronts sin with the law for the purpose of curing the guilt problem with the gospel.

God confronts sin with the law for the purpose of curing the guilt problem with the gospel. As our study continues, this particularly unique way of dealing with depression will become more obvious. God does not hesitate to confront guilty thoughts and feelings because he has the cure for guilt in the gospel of full and free forgiveness in Christ.

While secular psychology and psychiatry use tools such as medication and various forms of psychotherapy that we will consider, God uses those things along with his Word, both law and gospel, to free us from depression. God's tools and techniques are centered in the forgiveness and peace that Jesus won for us. Secular psychology and psychiatry are concerned with feelings and the ability to function. God is concerned about feelings, function, and our eternal welfare. That is easy to forget in the midst of depression. God's peace goes beyond time into eternity, without ignoring the needs we have now.

Suicide—a possible result of depression

The great prophet Elijah wanted to die after his awesome victory over the prophets of Baal. "He himself went a day's journey into the desert. He came to a broom tree, sat down under it and prayed that he might die. 'I have had enough, LORD,' he said. 'Take my life; I am no better than my ancestors'" (1 Kings 19:4).

Left unchecked, such thoughts in us can result in hopeless and faithless suicide. Suicide is a real danger when depression occurs, with the accompanying hopelessness it brings.

While Elijah only felt like giving up and dying, consider the following example:

> When Ahithophel saw that his advice had not been followed, he saddled his donkey and set out for his house in his hometown. He put his house in order and then hanged himself. So he died and was buried in his father's tomb (2 Samuel 17:23).

Without hope, especially the hope God provides, you may find it hard to believe life is worth living.

We also have the example of Judas: "Judas threw the money into the temple and left. Then he went away and hanged himself" (Matthew 27:5).

Judas had betrayed Jesus. Because he knew Jesus was innocent, he could see no reason for hope and no reason to want to live. Perhaps he thought he could atone for the life he had betrayed by taking his own life. Perhaps he thought that since he was guilty of murder, he deserved the death penalty. He was his own judge, jury, and executioner.

Regardless of the thoughts Judas had, the thought of hope in Christ's forgiveness was nowhere to be found. Judas died a hopeless and faithless man. Similarly, don't be surprised if you or someone you know leaves God out of the picture altogether when depression rules. Don't underestimate how dangerous depression can be, both physically and spiritually.

God's ways of dealing with depression

Scripture does provide examples of depressed people we can study for understanding and help. But we do better still to look at the central message of all Scripture. The central message of the Word of God is the unchanging faithful grace of God to a sinful, hurting, and dying world. That message addresses the needs of depressed people everywhere. The whole message is one of our guilt and God's grace centered in Jesus Christ. We will view the subject of

Don't underestimate how dangerous depression can be, both physically and spiritually.

depression in the light of God's law to show us our sin and the gospel of his saving and healing grace.

God's Word addresses depression as it does all other areas of our lives. God's law confronts the sin that can be the cause of depression. It shows you when something is wrong or missing in your relationship with God. By looking into the mirror of God's law you can recognize sin. Sin may be an act of disobedience. Sin may involve a missing element, something that you should have done and didn't. For example, if you fail or refuse to forgive as God requires, you will carry the weight of that neglected act of forgiveness.

The law will show you those sins. When you see them clearly you will also see your need to confess your guilt. That is the law's work.

The gospel, on the other hand, is the message of Christ's forgiveness for repentant sinners. You will find real resolution of the problem of guilt only in the good news about Jesus Christ and his work to save you. Scripture reveals that good news in the life, death, and resurrection of Christ. With that message you will find healing nothing else can provide.

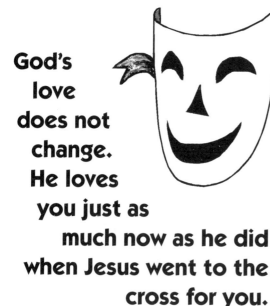

God's love does not change. He loves you just as much now as he did when Jesus went to the cross for you.

Sometimes depression doesn't go away. In some cases, unfortunately, depression is a way of life, perhaps the result of a physical ailment without a cure. God provides strength and hope for that reality too. God's love does not change. He loves you just as much now as he did when Jesus went to the cross for you. We all need to remember that love constantly, but especially when we must accept depression or any other lingering illness as a way of life.

Depression is not a reason for giving up on God. Depression does not mean that God has given up on you. Depression, like Paul's thorn in the flesh (2 Corinthians 12), is a reason for learning truths about God, his Word, and his will that we didn't know before. Our gracious God can use bad things to provide you with new insights into his love.

God tells you of his love in the Word, and he waits to hear you speak to him in prayer. Through prayer you can put yourself and your loved ones into God's caring hands. In depressing times, you may be more ready to listen to God and to talk with him. Depression offers a remarkable opportunity for that kind of conversation. God may actually provide a reason for a Christian to say thank you for the depression. "Thank you for the healing and peace and hope only Jesus could provide. I would not have seen it without the depression you used for my good."

Conclusion

Yes, Christians experience depression. No one is exempt from it. Christians, like everyone else, are sinful people living in a sinful world. Depression is one result of being sinners. As sinners, some of the ways we try to handle losses, anger, and guilt will prove to be mistakes. In that sense, Christians are no different from anyone else. But in another more important sense, we are different. Our relationship with God makes the difference. We have different tools for dealing with depression than others who don't know Christ and his Word. We have all the resources of secular psychology and psychiatry at our disposal. In addition, we have the holy Scriptures to provide an understanding of sin and grace in Christ. That is the most powerful tool of all.

Scripture provides us with a clear look at ourselves from God's point of view. It also provides us with a clear look at what God has done for us in his love. With God, overcoming depression is more than a matter of feeling better or functioning better; it is a matter of peace in Christ with a clear conscience and the assurance of God's love. Everyone needs that assurance and peace. If you are depressed, you may have more trouble seeing it and experiencing it than others. We want to help you see it better.

CHAPTER TWO

A Clinical Look at Depression

Who hasn't experienced the feeling of being sad, blue, or down in the dumps? Who hasn't had the experience of crying when a loss has occurred? Who hasn't had mood swings? Who hasn't experienced the emotional pain of living in a sinful world? Most people at one time or another have the feelings and thoughts that are often associated with depression.

Depression, as mentioned previously, is often referred to as the "Common Cold" of mental illness because it affects nearly everyone at some time. About five percent of the population suffers from a serious depression at any one time, and about ten percent of the population will at some point in their lives have a serious depression. Statistically, women are about twice as likely to experience depression as are men. Christians also, as normal, emotional beings, become depressed.

When Christians become depressed, they face a problem that can make depression even more difficult to deal with than usual. The Christian, on top of everything else, may think, "Why is God doing this to me?" "If only my faith were stronger, I wouldn't feel this way."

Sometimes well-meaning friends may say, "Look at all the blessings God has given to you. You shouldn't be depressed."

Or a friend may say, "You'll just have to put more trust in God."

Depressed persons may then be left with the feeling that they are doing something to bring on the depression. They may wonder: "Why won't God take these feelings away? What is he punishing me for? What am I doing wrong?"

These ideas bring on feelings of guilt: "I am doing something wrong. Something is wrong with me." Such thoughts only add to the depression. Such ideas suggest a lack of understanding about depression as well as a lack of understanding of how God deals with his children. As we consider depression from a clinical point of view, we will try to clear up these mistaken ideas.

Grief reactions

We all experience major losses: the loss of a spouse or child through death, the loss of a job, the loss of health, the feeling of loss with the breakup of a marriage by divorce, the feeling of loss at failing a test in school. All these events bring on feelings of sadness and perhaps even despair, but they are not the feelings of depression. For example, as Mary and Martha wept over the death of Lazarus, they were experiencing a normal, predictable, human feeling called a grief reaction. Grief reactions are not the same as depression. While they may be referred to as reactive depression, the grief reaction is part of the normal process of emotional adjustment that a person goes through when dealing with a specific loss.

Perhaps the following two examples will show how a reactive depression may occur:

Ever since the rumors of a possible plant closing began to circulate in the pressroom, Ralph has had difficulty getting a night of restful sleep. He awakens in the middle of the night with concern about his ability to find another job that will pay him enough to support his family. He worries about the loss of insurance and retirement benefits. What will happen to his family? Will they lose the house? What about college expenses? Ralph is spending more and more of his time and emotional energy agonizing over these questions.

• • • • • • •

It has been two weeks since Bill died. It all happened so fast. Only four weeks before he died, he learned he had an

---

inoperable tumor. No one, not even the doctors, thought it would go so fast! Janet is left with three children under ten, large medical bills, and a lot of unanswered questions. What hurts most is not having Bill nearby to rely on. Janet wonders how she will be able to survive without him. She wonders why God took Bill. It doesn't seem fair. God is supposed to be a loving God, not a God who takes a father away from his children. Why didn't God take her instead of Bill? She keeps hoping that she will awaken and find that this was all a bad dream.

Ralph and Janet are both experiencing grief reactions. Their reactions may resemble a depression, but they are different. While a grief reaction may at times trigger a depressive episode, usually it decreases in severity after a brief period. During this time, mourning is an appropriate spiritual and psychological response. Jesus said, "Blessed are those who mourn, for they will be comforted" (Matthew 5:4).

The person experiencing a grief reaction can be helped by supportive Christian friends who allow him or her to express feelings in an open and caring atmosphere. The grieving person needs friends who are able to listen and to reassure, in Christ, that God is still in control. Truly, "we know that in all things God works for the good of those who love him" (Romans 8:28). The Christian friend will want to be able to share the feelings of loss with the person in grief and through that sharing offer comfort and care. "Rejoice with those who rejoice; mourn with those who mourn" (Romans 12:15).

Major depression

While a grief reaction is a normal, predictable behavior that tends to resolve itself with time and spiritual care, the same is not true for actual depression. A major depression affects every part of a person's existence. It does not necessarily go away with time. It is also quite true that the emotional pain of depression may be worse than the physical pain one experiences with a physical illness.

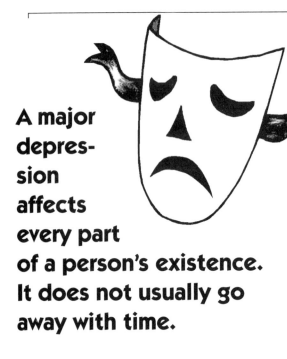

A major depression affects every part of a person's existence. It does not usually go away with time.

Lately it seems that Carol has been feeling "down" every day. No one thing is really bothering her; there's just a pervading sense of unhappiness. Even at work people have started to ask what is wrong. Carol is plagued by the idea that she is inferior to everyone and that even God is unhappy with her. While she knows of God's love and forgiveness, she doesn't feel the peace forgiveness brings. That causes her to wonder if perhaps she really doesn't believe anymore. At times she says she doesn't even have the energy to pray. Her sleep is not restful, and she is always nervous. As her depression increases, she experiences difficulties getting at her work and getting it done. That only adds to her depression. She is in a vicious downward cycle.

Carol is experiencing a major depression. She is being attacked on three fronts. Spiritual, psychological, and physical concerns are all affecting her. All three must be dealt with for her to feel better.

Brad just turned 16. He is a junior in high school. If anyone could be described as an "All American Boy," it would be Brad. He was always an above-average student and even had perfect attendance several years. He did well in sports and was usually considered to be a "neat guy" by his classmates. However, when Brad entered the ninth grade, he seemed to have some difficulty adjusting. The school was larger. He felt "out of place." He tried out for the basketball and baseball teams, but he didn't make the cut. In the tenth grade, his grades continued to drop. Brad started to become more isolated at school. For the first time in his school career, he started to skip classes. Now, in his junior year, he is failing several classes. He has no interest in school and no interest in sports. He is spending more time in his room alone, listening to music. He has considered suicide.

Although many would feel that the teenage years should be the best years of a person's life, for some teens these years can be very troublesome. Depression in teenagers is not always recognized as a depression because attention is drawn to the behavioral problems that are a result of the depression rather than the depression itself. It is not unusual for teens who are experiencing depression to begin to experiment with drugs and alcohol. They are looking for relief from their depressed feelings. Obviously, however, their involvement with drugs and alcohol only serves to make the problem worse.

Depression in teenagers is not always recognized as a depression because attention is drawn to the behavioral problems that are a result of the depression rather than the depression itself.

Carol and Brad are both suffering from depression. Although they behave quite differently from each other, their behaviors are influenced by depression. Simply telling Carol to "think only about happy things" or telling Brad to "get his act together" will not help. To better understand what is happening to Carol and Brad, it is necessary to know some of the basic characteristics of depression.

Characteristics of depression

Mood disturbances

Depression produces a total feeling of sadness that is not necessarily linked to any specific precipitating event. A person not only feels sad, he or she usually also appears sad. A depressed person may want to spend a great deal of time alone. The person may cry often and at times may seem unable to stop crying. Perhaps after time, the individual may say, "I can't even cry anymore."

At other times, the mood disturbance may go to the opposite direction of depression. The person may experience some extremely cheerful, euphoric periods. He may feel he has limitless physical energy. While at first glance it may appear that the individual has "snapped out" of the depression, the mood and actions will be seen as being excessive or "too high." After a short time, the euphoric feelings give way to the sadness, and the person falls back into the doldrums of depression.

Depression produces a total feeling of sadness that is not necessarily linked to any specific precipitating event.

Physical signs

Sleep disturbances are often a part of depression. Depressed persons often experience difficulty falling asleep because they can't relax. They may awaken early, unable to fall asleep again. Also, even though they have had sleep, they do not feel rested.

There may also be excessive amounts of sleep. Depressed persons may nap during the day even though there has been sufficient sleep time.

Appetite often changes. Depressed persons may become disinterested in food and not eat, or may eat excessively in an attempt to feel better. They may even gain or lose a significant amount of weight.

Headaches, digestive difficulties, and a decrease in sexual interest and performance often accompany depression.

Thought changes

Depressed persons often experience many negative thoughts about themselves. They may feel they are dumb, stupid, and worthless. They put themselves down and may feel that they just want to run and hide from everyone. In some forms of severe depression, the thinking may become delusional and irrational. Persons may lose touch with reality and may even experience auditory or visual hallucinations. If these severe symptoms occur, the person is in dire need of psychiatric intervention.

To the depressed person, life is "going through the motions."

Activity changes

The level of physical activity and stamina may decrease. Hobbies and outside interests lose their appeal. Even the day-to-day routine responsibilities may become overwhelming. The depressed person may begin to neglect personal appearance. He or she may withdraw from social interaction with friends and even family. To the depressed person, life is "going through the motions."

Increased anxiety

While sadness is the prevailing mood in depression, anxiety most often accompanies it. The anxious person becomes more irritable and restless. The increased anxiety may interfere with memory and concentration. Intellectual abilities that were commonplace before are no longer as easy to do. The person feels that if only he could relax, things would be better.

Thoughts of death

While certainly not all people who experience depression are suicidal, most have some thoughts about wishing to die. The thoughts of dying may come because the person feels of no value to others and may think, if not actually say, "They'd be better off without me." The wish to die may also come out of a sense of frustration, from the depressed persons not knowing of any way to stop the emotional pain they are experiencing. Even the depressed who are suicidal may not want to die; they just feel there is no other way to stop the hurting.

Guilt prone thinking

Depressed individuals often see themselves in a negative way because of an overwhelming sense of guilt. Depressed persons tend to become unusually introspective, but they see only faults and wrongs committed. They may begin to blame themselves for things over which they had no control. They may feel helpless and hopeless about ever recovering from the depression.

The Christian, in particular, may struggle with negative thinking. Christians are more inclined to be troubled about specific sins. Even though they have been assured that these sins have been forgiven, they do not "feel" forgiven. They may look at all the blessings God has given them and think, "How can I be depressed? Look what God has given to me." They feel guilty for being depressed. That only adds to the depression. They may have thoughts such

Only when the symptoms are so severe that they begin to interfere with routine, daily living is a diagnosis of depression made.

as, "If I prayed more, I'd overcome this." "God must be punishing me for something I did." Although Christians often experience these thoughts, they are not true. They are ways the devil uses to attack our sinful flesh.

Many people have experienced some of the above symptoms. Just because a person experiences one or two of them, however, does not necessarily mean the person is depressed. We always need to look at the number of symptoms and the severity of the symptoms. Remember, everyone will have some of these feelings in daily life. Only when the symptoms are so severe that they begin to interfere with routine, daily living is a diagnosis of depression made. The best way to evaluate the number and severity of symptoms is to consult a competent Christian counselor. He or she will be able to put the symptoms into a proper perspective and make a proper diagnosis.

Specific types of depression

As has been stated previously, not all depression is the same. Obviously, the type of depression will determine the necessary treatment. In order to provide insight into the forms of depression, the following descriptions are provided:

Reactive depression

Clinically speaking, this is not considered a specific category of depression. As described earlier, this is the "downer" most people experience at one time or another in their lives. This is a depressive reaction in response to a particular precipitating factor such as a major loss. The person will experience some of the symptoms of depression that were described above, but this reaction tends to be of a shorter duration.

Manic-depressive illness

This is also referred to as a bipolar disorder. Basically there are two types of bipolar disorders. In one type, the manic or high state is the predominant feature, while the depressive or low state is the predominant feature in the other. In a manic-depressive illness, the person's moods will change from one extreme to the other, high to low and back again or vice versa. This type of depression has a strong hereditary factor that seems to predispose some people to it. This type of illness is quite treatable with medication.

In the manic state, the person may display high levels of physical energy, feelings of euphoria, and a great deal of impulsiveness that surfaces in acts of poor judgment. In this state, the person may have endless energy and may accomplish a great deal of work. Unfortunately, manic people may also take financial risks and display other inappropriate behaviors.

In the depressed state, the person will experience many of the depressed symptoms previously described.

Cyclothymic disorder

This disorder is often looked upon as being a "lesser" form of manic-depressive illness. It is called cyclothymic ("cycling mind") because it involves alternating periods of lively and depressed moods. This condition does not involve the impairment in daily functioning that the manic-depressive illness does. Frequently, drug and alcohol addiction may be associated with this condition because the person is trying to "self-medicate."

Major depression, single episode or recurrent

This type of depression may also be referred to as unipolar depression. This condition is characterized by a major depressive episode without a manic phase. Such a depressive episode may occur only one time, or it may be a recurring episode. In its more severe form, the person with a major depression has a difficult time in maintaining a normal day-to-day schedule. The various symptoms that were described previously may take a heavy toll on such persons and limit their daily activities.

Dysthymic disorder

Dysthymia means literally "bad mind." This condition was originally referred to as a neurotic depression. It is often seen as a "lesser" form of depression. It involves a chronic depressed mood, but not of sufficient severity to drastically affect daily living.

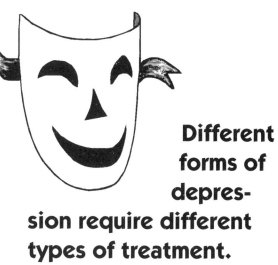

Different forms of depression require different types of treatment.

Psychotic depression

Psychosis is a serious mental disorder in which the ability to deal with reality is impaired or lost. In this extreme condition, the person has all of the symptoms of a severe depression. In addition, he is also experiencing auditory or visual hallucinations. Hallucinations are beliefs that the person is able to see or hear things that no one else is able to experience.

Depression secondary to other physical illness

In this condition the depressive episode is brought about by some other sickness such as cancer, diabetes, or heart trouble. Sometimes depression may be the side-effect of certain medications used to treat other illnesses.

With this knowledge about the different types of depression, one should be better able to understand the various factors and conditions related to depression. Different forms of depression require different types of treatment.

TEST YOURSELF

Do you wonder whether you or someone you know is suffering from depression? The following brief test can help you determine for sure. You can answer the questions yourself if you are feeling depressed. You can encourage someone else to answer them. If necessary, you can try to answer them the way you think someone you care about might answer them. The answers you give will help you decide what kind of help you should be seeking, how much you need help, and how soon you need to obtain it. Depression is a problem that can have both a clinical side and a spiritual side. You can't really separate the two, but it is hoped you will find some guidance for obtaining the help that will be most beneficial.

Answer true or false to the following statements. If the statements do not seem to apply directly, answer them false. If they seem to apply some or most of the time, mark them true.

_____ 1. I feel sad and unhappy more than I feel happy.

_____ 2. I often feel like crying.

_____ 3. I often feel my life is hopeless and I am helpless to make any changes in my life.

_____ 4. I tend to view myself as a failure and a disappointment to those who know me.

_____ 5. Frequently I feel bad and guilty, and I feel a need to be punished.

_____ 6. I believe that I am less of a person now than I was a year ago.

_____ 7. Things just don't interest me anymore.

_____ 8. I seldom get excited and happy about anything.

_____ 9. There are days when I have to force myself to do the things I need to do.

_____ 10. My moods seem to go "up and down" for no reason.

_____ 11. I am finding it more and more difficult to make decisions.

_____ 12. I have a difficult time concentrating on things.

_____ 13. At times I feel that life is just too painful to keep living.

_____ 14. I am not as particular about my physical appearance as I used to be.

_____ 15. My sleeping patterns have changed. I am sleeping significantly more or less than I used to.

_____ 16. My appetite has changed. I am eating significantly more or less than I used to.

_____ 17. I often feel extra tired. My energy level is very low.

_____ 18. I am spending more time worrying than I used to.

_____ 19. I am overcritical of myself.

_____ 20. I find myself wondering about and at times even doubting God's love for me.

If you feel that the majority of the preceding statements are presently true for you and not likely to change, you are probably experiencing depression and should seek professional help. The more items you marked true, the more urgent it is for you to seek help that is available.

CHAPTER THREE

How Depression Is Treated

The person who admits he or she is experiencing depression has already taken a positive step in the recovery process. He is acknowledging he has a problem. This is a positive step because depression is a condition that responds well to treatment.

The effective treatment program for depression will take into account the physical, emotional, and spiritual dimensions that must be considered for effective treatment. To view depression as a single-cause condition and thus make use of a single treatment denies the complexity of the condition and the interaction of the physiological, psychological, and spiritual components.

Unfortunately, all too often the person experiencing depression is told: "Snap out of it." "Pull yourself together." "Think only about happy things." "Count

What a depressed person needs to hear is "I care about you and want to help," "God will continue to help you through this," or "I really want to know how you are feeling."

your blessings." More likely than not, such comments will only add to the depression the person is feeling because these comments imply that *it is your fault* that you are depressed.

What a depressed person needs to hear is "I care about you and want to help," "God will continue to help you through this," or "I really want to know how you are feeling."

Physiological understandings and treatment of depression

Depression in women

Research consistently shows that women are more likely to experience depression than men. Some argue, however, that the different rates for depression in men and women reflect merely that women are more willing to admit to being depressed than are men. It is generally true that women are more likely to seek help for any type of problem they are having. Men usually tend to be more defensive and more reluctant to go for outside help.

This factor, however, does not account for the differences in the rate of depression between men and women. Before menstruation a woman's body chemistry seems to undergo particular changes that are associated with mood changes. The change in estrogen and progesterone levels at this time are known to affect the central nervous system, which may bring about feelings of depression. This phenomenon, known as the premenstrual syndrome (PMS), may contribute significantly to women experiencing depression in a regular cyclic pattern.

In this condition, the woman usually has feelings of depression and anxiety, beginning about a week before her period. During that time the feelings become more pronounced until she begins her period. Then the symptoms decrease. Women who experience this kind of pattern to their depression should consult their physician about treatment. The use of some dietary considerations and perhaps medication can help in dealing with this type of depression.

Postpartum depression is another form of depression that is unique to women. This depression may occur up to two years after the birth of a child. While it is sometimes believed that the cause for this type of depression is the body's reaction to the physiological changes that occurred during pregnancy, another cause may be rooted in the mother's mixed feelings about the pregnancy and the responsibility of raising a child. In this type of depression, a woman commonly has strong fears that she is going to bring harm to her baby. When these feelings are not talked about but are kept in, they usually become more severe. The new mother who is able to talk about these concerns is doing much to deal effectively with such fears.

Women also commonly experience a degree of depression at menopause. While it has usually been believed that this depression occurred because of a lack of estrogen production, some researchers question that assumption. Perhaps a more valid explanation for menopause is that at this time in a woman's life she may be dealing with various losses. For some women, the loss of the ability to bear more children may be a major factor. They may associate that loss with a perceived loss of attractiveness, sexuality, and feeling of youthfulness. At that point the woman may see her life in terms of what she is not able to do instead of what opportunities still lie ahead for her.

Besides the three specific conditions referred to above, which are unique to women, there still appears to be a greater likelihood for women to experience depression than men. Whether or not this is biological in nature or perhaps a factor of our society is not really known.

There is a bio-logical and genetic factor in depression.

Biology and depression

There is a biological and genetic factor in depression. We need to know this so that we can better understand what depression is and how it can be treated. As God has given us gifts of understanding and healing, we want to be able to apply that knowledge to depression.

Any thought we have, any emotion we experience, any memory we store, and any action we take are the result of electrochemical reactions that occur in the central nervous system and in the brain specifically. All of this takes place as impulses cause the nerves to release chemicals that are called neurotransmitters. The purpose of the neurotransmitters is to transmit an electrical impulse from one neuron through a space called the synaptic gap to the next neuron. As the neurotransmitter is released by one neuron, it is taken into the next neuron.

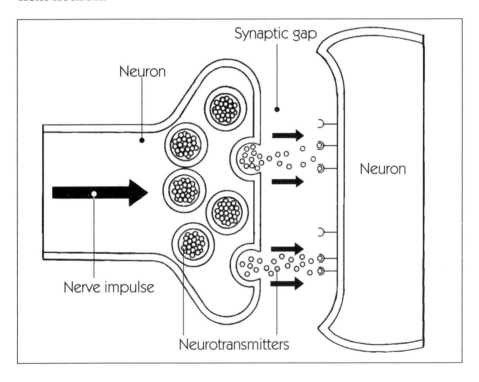

In this process, the electrical impulse is carried through the nervous system. Back at the nerve site, however, the neurotransmitter that was received by one neuron must be sent back to the sending neuron. It is at this point, where the neurotransmitters are sent out, absorbed, and then sent back for reuse, that a "chemical imbalance" may occur. It is theorized that two specific neurotransmitters, mainly norepine-phrine (noradrenalin) and serotonin, if underproduced or overproduced, can bring a biologically based depression.

While this entire process is obviously quite complex, we can understand from it that there is a biological aspect to depression. For many people who feel guilty over being depressed, this knowledge can be quite comforting because it shows them that there is a biological link to their depression. This knowledge may lessen their guilt feelings about depression and help them gain a better understanding about it. This type of depression is usually referred to as an endogenous depression (coming from within) as opposed to an exogenous depression (coming from outside). It is for this endogenous depression, where there is what might be termed faulty functioning of the neurotransmitters, that the use of antidepressant medication can be of much help.

The most common types of antidepressant medications are referred to as tricyclic antidepressants. Some of the common tricyclics by trade name are Elavil, Asendin, Norpramin, Sinequan, Tofranil, and Pamelor. Some typical side effects from these medications may be drowsiness, blurred vision, dry mouth, and light-headedness. These are more commonly used than are antidepressants referred to as monamine oxidase inhibitors or MAOIs. The commonly used MAOIs are Marplan, Nardil, and Parnate. Individuals taking any of these medications usually need to avoid certain kinds of foods such as aged cheese and yogurt.

The antidepressant medications can be quite

The anti-depressant medications can be quite effective in greatly reducing the symptoms of depression.

effective in greatly reducing the symptoms of depression. Sometimes the physician will have to adjust the dosage in order to get it to a therapeutic level. Also, it may take about two or three weeks before the medication is able to bring about the desired effect.

Another medication that helps greatly in the treatment of depression is lithium. This is the medication most frequently used for those suffering from a bipolar disorder (manic depression), and it carries a very high success rate.

In order to investigate the possibility of a biological basis for depression, one needs to consult with a physician. Often a general practitioner or a family physician will refer an individual to a psychiatrist. Sometimes people may feel offended or frightened if they are referred to a psychiatrist, because often a person does not understand the function of a psychiatrist. Psychiatry is the branch of medicine that deals with the relationship between bodily functioning and mental health. A psychiatrist will have information about what physical causes may be bringing on a depression and will also be able to prescribe appropriate medication for the condition.

In order to investigate the possibility of a biological basis for depression, one needs to consult with a physician.

Depression and electroconvulsive therapy (ECT)

Electroconvulsive therapy, also referred to as electroshock treatment, is a treatment for those individuals who are suffering from severe depression, psychotic depression, or for those who have made serious suicide attempts while depressed. For those with severe depression who require the use of substantial medication, ECT may have many fewer side effects. In historical perspective, ECT has received much negative reaction. Today, however, it is believed to be a safe and effective treatment for the more severely depressed person.

Genetics and depression

It has become quite clear that genetic factors play a part in determining the likelihood of someone being depressed. (It is genetics that determines the color hair and eyes one has.) It is believed that certain people have a genetic predisposition to become depressed. This does not mean that they will be depressed, but rather it means they are more likely to become depressed than others because of their genetic makeup. The predisposition seems to be particularly true in a major depressive illness and in manic depression. Realizing that there may be a genetic link to depression may help an individual to better understand and accept his depressive condition.

Psychological understanding and treatment of depression

Now that we have looked at the physiological components of depression, we want to look at the various psychological components of depression. No one particular psychological factor causes a person to become depressed. It cannot be said, for instance, that because this particular event took place in this individual's life that he will become depressed. It is also not accurate to say that there is a depressive personality type. Depression may occur in any of the various personality types that researchers have identified.

In order to understand better the psychological factors leading to depression, it often helps to picture depression as being more likely to occur as people experience various losses in their lives. And the younger one is when these losses occur, the more traumatic they may become. As the following list of losses is presented, however, it does not mean that everyone who is depressed has experienced each loss. Nor is it intended to say that a person who experiences one of these losses will become depressed. As God has made us all different, he has also given us different abilities to cope with the stresses in daily life.

It often helps to picture depression as being more likely to occur as people experience various losses in their lives.

Loss of love

Probably one of the most difficult things for a person to experience is a loss of love or a conditional type of love. A child may be raised without love at home because he or she is seen as an extra burden for the parents. Perhaps the parents are too busy with their own lives or careers to show love for the child. Perhaps the child learns to believe that he is only loved when he is getting good grades or honors at school. Or maybe the child is brought up with the thought, "Jesus doesn't love you when you do that." In adolescence, that loss of love may occur when a romantic relationship suddenly comes to an end. In adults, the loss of love may take place when a marriage relationship disintegrates and family closeness disappears. How important it is to know that we can never lose God's love!

Loss of self-esteem

Because of God's great love for us in sending a Savior for our sins, we now have worth through Christ. We have value because we are children of God through faith in Christ. Nevertheless it is possible to lose all sense of worth and become depressed.

What about the child who grows up in a home where he or she is constantly criticized? His shortcomings are always pointed out, but his accomplishments are never recognized. When the child feels he has finally been successful and earned the love of the parents, he finds that the expectations have been raised to a new high.

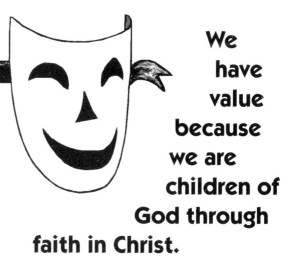

We have value because we are children of God through faith in Christ.

How can the child who is physically or emotionally abused by a parent escape the feeling that "I'm bad; something is wrong with me"? Or how can the child who has been sexually abused by a parent escape from the self-imposed shame that is a part of that abuse? These losses of self-esteem may also occur in adults. The spouse ridicules or constantly "puts down" the mate. The spouse physically abuses the mate. The spouse who finds that the mate has been "cheating" on her will very likely blame herself with statements such as "I'm not good enough for him."

The above serve as examples of events that may occur in an individual's life which may easily bring on feelings of worthlessness and depression. While obviously our true worth comes from what Christ has done for us, these traumatic experiences in life from individuals who were loved and trusted can make it difficult to experience the feelings of worth in being children of God.

Loss of emotional intimacy

Everyone—adult, adolescent, or child—needs to have an intimate emotional relationship. Such a relationship lets the person know that he is cared about and that another person has his best interests at heart. Husbands and wives are to develop this intimate relationship in their marriage when they leave their parental home and "become one flesh" (Genesis 2:24). The unmarried usually find this intimate relationship in personal friendships or other personal relationships. A friendship like the one that existed between Jonathan and David or the closeness between Ruth and her mother-in-law Naomi demonstrates the feeling of emotional intimacy. The lack of such an intimate relationship brings on feelings of isolation and loneliness, which often lead to depression.

Loss of control or direction

Anxiety is always a part of depression. Anxiety results when persons feel that they are losing the ability to take control of the events going on in their lives.

Anxiety is always a part of depression.

Anxiety may result when persons find out that they are about to lose their jobs. A woman especially may experience anxiety from the "empty nest" syndrome. As the loss of control becomes greater, the person begins to feel helpless in taking control of his or her life and may begin to feel hopeless.

Loss of an intimate relationship with God

As individuals neglect to nurture their relationship with God, they begin to feel isolated from him. Feelings of forsakenness and alienation set in. If the person allows these feelings to continue without returning to God, he or she is left feeling unloved and uncared for. When we remain in Christ, he will remain in us, and thus we are not alone. "I am the vine; you are the branches. If a man remains in me and I in him, he will bear much fruit" (John 15:5).

The above are just some of the psychological factors that may play a part in one's depression. While none of these may actually bring on a depression, the accumulation of them will certainly increase the likelihood of one becoming depressed.

Helping one in need

As such losses occur, one needs to develop a strategy for effectively dealing with them. Often we can do this in an intimate relationship where one is able freely to open his or her heart of concern. This relationship allows for the opportunity to "please [one's] neighbor for his good, to build him up" (Romans 15:2). The question may often arise, however, "What do I tell a person who is depressed?" Perhaps the best way to learn of a way to help a person going through depression is to read the account of Jesus counseling the two disciples on the way to Emmaus (Luke 24:13-35). As one reads this account, specific techniques are seen that can also be applied to present-day settings.

1. First Jesus showed compassion for the men. He wanted to help them. The effective helper will have an attitude of love, compassion, and empathy. However, merely showing pity or sympathy is not a productive way to help work through problems. Be sincere in your desire to help rather than curious about what is wrong.

A good listener is one who not only listens to the words being said, but also listens to the feelings behind these words.

2. Second, Jesus got them to talk about their concerns while he listened.

Much of the helping process revolves around being a good listener. A good listener is one who not only listens to the words being said, but also listens to the feelings behind these words. Avoid comments like "You shouldn't feel that way" or "This is what I would do." Also, don't trivialize a person's comments with statements such as "I know just how you feel." James gives the advice that "Everyone should be quick to listen, slow to speak" (James 1:19).

3. After listening comes some instructing. In friendship counseling, the instructing may take the form of helping the individual gain a better understanding of his or her concern. It may also take the form of encouraging the individual to seek out more professional help so the person is able to obtain an accurate diagnosis of the condition.

For most people who experience depression, some form of counseling or psychotherapy may be helpful. This counseling may take different formats and may be provided by different professions. The more traditional therapies are as follows:

1. Pastoral counseling can help the person with depression understand the spiritual aspects of depression. This counseling can also provide the individual with all of the spiritual help and comfort offered through God's Word.

2. What might be referred to as talking therapy—also referred to as psychotherapy—helps the depressed individual to change and adjust his negative thought processes. Talking about one's concerns helps the person to gain insight into why he has come to have the feelings he has. A psychotherapist is also able to offer suggestions on how to change the self-destructing thought cycle. Psychotherapy tends to be quite effective in treating the mild and moderate forms of depression.

3. Behavior therapy works on the principle that one must change certain behavior patterns in order to allevi-

ate depression. One is encouraged to perform the typical behaviors that were done in the nondepressed state. The belief is that nondepressed behaviors will bring about nondepressed thinking.

4. A specific form of psychotherapy referred to as psychodynamic therapy makes the assumption that the feelings of depression are rooted in the unresolved personal conflicts that took place in childhood. It is believed that as the conflicts are examined and better understood, they can be resolved. The resolution of these conflicts are believed to decrease the feelings of depression.

CHAPTER FOUR

The Spiritual Roots of Depression

We have discussed some of the ways depression shows itself. We considered a variety of types of depression as well as various ways to deal with it. One of the most common characteristics of a depressed person is a feeling of alienation. He or she is likely to feel alienated from people. The person will also likely feel far away from God.

Let's imagine that Jane has been feeling very low emotionally. Her appetite has soared and so has her weight. She has found it difficult to fall asleep at night. If she finally gets to sleep, she finds it is almost impossible to get up in the morning. Even the most basic tasks are more than she can handle. It's a chore to get lunches for the children and to make the beds. The only thing she has the energy to do is to turn on the television and watch it all day—as long as the remote control is working. Her doctor has prescribed medication for depression.

Jane has begun to wonder where God fits into all of this. If God were really a caring God, she thinks, he should see to it that the medication would help. She is beginning to become bitter toward God and people too. Someone should be able to help. Someone should care enough to help. Or perhaps Jane thinks she should be able to work it all out by herself with a little help from God. After all, she is a Christian, and Christians shouldn't feel this way. Where is God when you really need him?

God is always deeply involved in our lives, and he is involved where depression is concerned too. In this chapter we want to consider how he is involved. If there is a medical or physical cause for the depression, does that mean you have no need to turn to God for strength, direction, and the continuing assurance of his faithful love? If there is a spiritual problem, a problem such as guilt, anger toward someone else, or anger turned inward, how does God resolve things like that?

A closer look at depression

One of the most dangerous aspects of depression is the feeling of alienation from people and from God. That feeling is usually a part of the depression itself. In spiritual terms, depression is a self-centered disorder. It is a vicious cycle. If you ask the depressed how they feel, they will usually tell you, "I feel bad." Now look at those words this way.

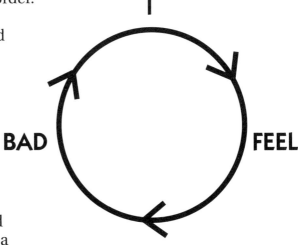

Looking within themselves, depressed people tend to magnify and to "feed on" their bad feelings. They spend a great deal of time thinking about themselves. If you are constantly thinking about yourself, you will naturally think about the way you feel. When you think about the way you feel, the bad feelings will dominate. The bad feelings will, then, prompt more thinking about yourself. As the cycle continues, you will find yourself thinking more and more about yourself and the bad feelings you have. Consequently, your feelings will become worse. Finally, you can only see how bad you feel. From that point of view, everything else looks bad too.

Looking within themselves, depressed people tend to magnify and to "feed on" their bad feelings.

When Jane felt depressed, she concentrated on how she felt. It didn't matter what anyone else said to her, she knew what was happening to her. She was the authority on the subject of how she felt, no one else. The more she thought about herself, the more she thought about how bad she felt. The feelings were all bad. No one else, not even God, fit into that picture. No one else could understand because she was the authority on her own feelings. She would not allow input from anyone else.

In that vicious cycle she also started making judgments about God. For example, she knew God was loving, yet she didn't feel loved. She concluded that while God might be a loving God, he certainly didn't love her. She had faith, so she reasoned that her faith should be able to bring her through all this. But it wasn't working. Something must be wrong with her faith. Her faith must have been weaker than anyone else's, otherwise she wouldn't feel the way she did. She knew that no one can get along without God, yet Jane thought that she SHOULD be able to get along by herself. In truth, no Christian reaches a point where he or she SHOULD be able to get along without God. But Jane didn't see it that way.

Depression has a way of magnifying all these feelings the depressed person has and leaving God and everyone else out of the picture. Satan likes nothing better than that.

A popular poem called "Footprints" expresses a similar thought:

One night a man had a dream. He dreamed he was
walking along the beach with the Lord.
Across the sky flashed scenes from his life.
For each scene he noticed two sets of footprints
in the sand: one belonged to him, and the other to the Lord.

When the last scene of his life flashed before him,
he looked back at the footprints in the sand.
He noticed that many times along the path of his life
there was only one set of footprints.
He also noticed that
it happened at
the very lowest and
saddest times in
his life.

This really
bothered
him and he
questioned the
Lord about it. "Lord,
you said that once
I followed
you, you'd walk with
me all the way.
But I have noticed
that during the
most troublesome
times in my life
there is only one
set of footprints.

She knew that no one can get along without God, yet Jane thought that she SHOULD be able to get along by herself.

"I don't understand why when I needed you most
you would leave me."
The Lord replied, "My precious, precious child,
I love you and I would never leave you during
your times of trial and suffering. When you see
only one set of footprints,
it was then that I carried you."

Author unknown

51

In the poem, the man saw a time in his life when only one set of footprints appeared in the sand. Those footprints appeared during the times that were the hardest and most difficult for him. His conclusion was that those low times in his life were times when God deserted him. In truth, however, as the poem points out, those were the times when the man was so weak that God had to carry him.

When you see only one set of footprints, it was then that I carried you.

Depression causes the kind of lonely feeling that "Footprints" talks about. Although God always has a place in our lives as believers, in depression, he often seems either far away or gone from our lives altogether. A depressed person is likely to turn away from God and stay in the depressed state or else try to find some cure for it without God.

But, if there is to be any true peace, God must fit into the picture. At a time like that, a competent and concerned Christian friend needs to remind the depressed person patiently that God has not left him or her alone at all. We must be ready to assure a depressed person that God's love is unchanging love. His power is almighty power. His care, concern, forgiveness, and peace will never depart. What changes is our ability to see those unchanging facts clearly.

Depression is a spiritual matter

A depressed person is not likely to seek God's answers to the problem of depression. He or she needs to be led back to the faithful love of God. But what then? Jane's problem might have been a physical or medical problem. Perhaps a chemical imbalance caused her depression, and she requires medication to help her deal with it. Does God fit into that scenario too?

Of course he does. Whenever we face earthly matters that threaten our well-being, we need God. At the very least, as with an impending surgery, we need the comfort and assurance of God's continued love, presence, and blessing. We need to place our care and healing in his hands. We need to confess our sins and receive his forgiveness. We still use the surgeon, but we bring God with us.

Whenever we face earthly matters that threaten our well-being, we need God.

The same thing is true with depression. We may need professional treatment and have to live with continued medication, but we bring God with us.

Sometimes God teaches his people to depend on him to be able to endure a difficult problem like depression. Let's imagine that Jane has found out that her depression is the result of a chemical imbalance that requires medication for the rest of her life. On hearing that prognosis, she is naturally disappointed. After all, she felt bad enough before she knew what the problem was. Now it's even worse. She will have to accept the best that this medicine or some other treatment can provide. It may not make her feel much better. She needs to know that God will keep her in his care through it all.

Not many people would like living with depression. But God can use the depression as a test to strengthen faith. He also promises us that he will not desert us when we are so tested.

You might justifiably ask how something like depression can make a Christian's faith stronger. Simply put, when you feel the weakest, then God's strength means the most. When depression leaves you without any hope, God is your hope. Depression is a destructive disorder. Only God can make something so devastating accomplish a strengthening purpose.

If you wonder how that works, look at the case of the Apostle Paul. He had a problem, a "thorn in [his] flesh," that would not go away. Although he asked God three times to take it away, God's answer was no (see 2 Corinthians 12:7-10). God had good reason for not taking that thorn in the flesh away. It helped Paul learn to find his strength in Christ rather than in himself.

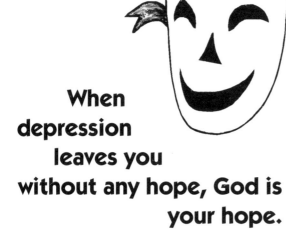

When depression leaves you without any hope, God is your hope.

A thorn causes pain. Pain, whether it is emotional or physical, is a reminder that we are human beings. When we can't make the pain go away, it reminds us of our human limitations. We soon realize that we are not self-sufficient. We are constantly dependent on God and his grace. Even the great missionary Paul needed that reminder.

When people are depressed, they will likely need help to understand and appreciate the importance of God's saving grace. From a depressed person's point of view, life is bad, he or she is worthless, and God is far away. Satan loves to perpetuate that lie. A concerned friend, Christian counselor, or pastor who knows the faithful love and power of Jesus can help. Such a person can confront sin as needed and bring comfort and forgiveness in Christ.

When you know that the vision of your depressed friend is limited, perhaps to the point of seeing only bad things, you can provide the vision of God's love that tells the truth. As a Christian, you have more to offer than sympathy and compassion. You know the unchanging love of God that works even when things look bad. Drawing on Paul's experience, you might even say that God's love and strength show the best when things look the worst.

We have considered the possibility that Jane may be depressed about being depressed. She seems to feel that Christians just SHOULDN'T get depressed, and she wonders what is wrong with her faith. We know that she may be inclined to find help apart from considering her relationship with God. We know that she needs support from people who know and love her. But she especially needs help from people who know and love Christ and can share his support with her. We will be discussing further the kind of help Christian friends can give.

We soon realize that we are not self-sufficient.

Guilty, angry, and depressed

Let's see how guilt and anger might be playing a serious part in Jane's depression. Often, guilt and anger can be the root of the depression.

Consider this familiar situation: During the late years in her life, Jane's mother was very difficult to deal with. Her thinking was not always clear. She was demanding and manipulative. Jane was often angry with her and resented the demands that made Jane feel as if she could never do enough to please her mother.

When her mother became seriously ill, was hospitalized, and was seldom conscious, Jane felt compelled to be by her side constantly, even though her mother never realized Jane was there. Day and night Jane was by her side. Then, when Jane left the room for a few minutes to get some coffee, her mother quietly passed away.

God's love and strength show the best when things look the worst.

The loss of her mother was a significant loss in itself. Jane felt the grief of a daughter who has just lost her mother. In addition, however, Jane felt guilty about the anger she harbored toward her mother. Jane had never been able to resolve that anger by talking it through with her. Her mother's mental condition didn't allow that. Besides, when her mother was unconscious, Jane had been hoping for a moment just to be able to tell her she was sorry. That was the reason Jane never left the room. But she never had the opportunity to talk to her mother again. To make matters worse, she wasn't even there when her mother died. The lady died alone in a hospital room. No family members or friends were with her.

A situation like this is loaded with potential for depression. In a sense, the depression had nothing to do with Jane's loss of her mother. It was completely (selfishly) wrapped up in Jane's feelings about her relationship with her mother. Jane was angry with her mother for treating her the way she did. She was angry with God for allowing her mother to lapse into the condition she was in. The Lord took her before Jane had the opportunity to make things right. She was angry with herself for not being more understanding. She felt guilty for being so selfish that a cup of coffee was more important than being with her mother during her last moments of life.

You may wonder why such thoughts should cause a deep depression for Jane. After all, what could Jane have done differently? She reacted the way most normal human beings would react. She did the best she could. Yes, she did, but most of us know that thoughts and feelings of anger and guilt like these, as unreasonable as they may seem, still cause a great deal of pain and grief to those who experience them. Without even realizing it, people can live with such memories, with feelings of anger and guilt, all suppressed for years. Depression may often be the result.

Most of us know that thoughts and feelings of anger and guilt like these, as unreasonable as they may seem, still cause a great deal of pain and grief to those who experience them.

Am I at the root of my own depression?

We are examining the spiritual roots of depression. We have considered the self-centeredness of depression, the anger that is turned inward, and the guilty feelings. Have we really reached the root of the problem? Can we boil this down to even simpler terms that we can use to understand depression and deal with it effectively? I think we can. The terms can be made even simpler. Consider for a moment that all of these feelings are centered on the individual. Jane and Jane alone had the feelings.

In addition, Jane had feelings that required much more than she was able to give. Jane tried to cope with all the problems alone. Depressed people often do that. Jane thought she should have been able to leave the guilty feelings behind. All she could do was suppress them. She thought she should have known when her mother was going to die. She thought she should have been there when it happened.

All of the problems were a result of trying to do God's job instead of letting God do what only he can do.

In her problems, Jane succumbed to one fatal flaw. She was trying to do God's work. All of the problems were a result of trying to do God's job instead of letting God do what only he can do. God determines when life begins and ends, not people. God is present everywhere at all times, not people. Only God can provide real forgiveness, not people.

Understanding the difference between God's work and ours is an important factor in emotional and spiritual health. Often people try to do God's work for him and then complain to him or about him when problems arise. We will understand the spiritual root of depression when we properly understand the First Commandment: "You shall have no other gods" (Exodus 20:3).

God expects us to fear, love, and trust in him above all things. Other things, other people, even our own selves must take their places after God. More than anything else, Jane needed a concerned and loving Christian friend, pastor, or counselor to point out that the god in her life was not the true God. She was trying to be her own god.

Her depression showed her how difficult her life could be without God. She couldn't forgive herself. She needed God to do that. She couldn't do everything she expected of herself. And she couldn't accept what God was doing with her life because she had her own ideas of what "God" would do in her circumstances.

You would think that confronting Jane with all this would not only be a difficult thing to do, but that it would be devastating to her. She is depressed already. Won't talking like this depress her even more? While a Christian friend or counselor would not want to use

We will understand the spiritual root of depression when we properly understand the First Commandment: "You shall have no other gods."

these thoughts to attack Jane and her depression, a patient and loving presentation of God's law serves to show God's people the real problem. Then, healing can begin.

A patient and loving presentation of God's law serves to show God's people the real problem. Then, healing can begin.

Jane's pastor realized that things weren't right in her life after her mother died, so eventually they talked. The desired results didn't come instantly, but they did come. Over a period of time, the discussion took the following course:

Pastor (P): Jane, you haven't seemed like yourself lately. I hardly see you out with anyone. You've stopped coming to Bible class. Half the time you aren't even in church. That's just not like you. I can't help feeling something's wrong.

Jane (J): I know, Pastor, but I don't know what to say. It's not that I don't want to talk about it, I just don't know what to say. There's nothing I can do about the way I feel.

P: You may be right, but let's at least talk about it. When did you start feeling the way you do?

J: I know it sounds silly, but it happened about two months after my mother died. I can't think of any reason why I should feel this way. My mother was so hard to deal with. She made life miserable for me for a long time. (Jane starts to cry.)

P: It looks to me like she still is making life miserable for you. Do you know what is making you cry?

J: No, I really don't. I should be happy to have the freedom I have now, but I just feel miserable.

P: Maybe your mother didn't have as much to do with making you miserable as you think. Is it possible that you were letting her make you miserable?

J: She always demanded so much. I was always supposed to be there. I was always supposed to be able to do the right things. I was always supposed to . . .

P: Are you saying that your mother wanted you to play God?

J: That's exactly what she did. She wanted me to be God.

P: What did you do about that?

J: I tried to do the best I could to satisfy her demands.

P: Think about that for a moment. Who really wanted you to be God? Was it your mother or was it you who wanted to be God?

J: What could I do? She was constantly asking for more.

P: Do you think you might have made a mistake in dealing with those demands the way you did?

J: I don't know what you mean. She was my mother.

P: I mean that you could have said no to her.

J: Nobody got away with saying no to my mother.

P: What I'm trying to say is that even though your mother was trying to make you do God's job, the real problem is that you believed you could do the job. Is that why I never visited your mother without finding you there? Is that why you kept telling me that you should have been with her when she died?

J: I never believed I could do God's job, but I guess I was trying. I just feel so bad about the way I treated her for so long. I ignored her. I found other things to do instead of being with her. I wasn't always kind to her when we talked.

P: Do you think you're going to be able to pay for all that by being miserable? Your mother isn't making you miserable; you're doing it to yourself.

J: I guess I can see that, but I don't know what to do about it.

P: I'm sure you don't. All of us try to play God more often than we think. The problem is that the time comes to realize that God is God and we aren't. I think now is the time for you to realize that.

J: What could God do to fix a mess like this? I've been carrying this messed-up thinking around with me for months, and nothing I do seems to help make it go away.

P: Maybe that's because you're not God. You are only trying to be God, and it's not working. God can do a better job as God than you can. Just think about that for a moment. The best you can do to repair all this damage is to be miserable. You know that isn't God's way of handling the problem. How would God handle a sin like this?

J: Maybe he'll help me carry it.

P: No, that's not God's way. He didn't promise to help you make up for your sins. What is God's way?

J: His way was to let Jesus carry them instead of me.

P: That's the whole point, isn't it? He carried it so that you wouldn't have to. He didn't promise to help you carry this weight; he promised to carry it in your place. That's what all the pain and suffering on the cross was about. I can see how bad you feel, but it isn't paying for anything. When Jesus experienced all his misery and suffering, it did accomplish something. He did it to take your misery and suffering away.

J: Do you mean this miserable feeling can go away eventually?

P: I mean it can go away right now because Jesus is talking to you right now. Do you remember what he said on the cross before he died?

J: He said a lot of things, but what comes to mind right now is, "It is finished."

P: Those are the words I'm talking about. It's a sin to try to make anyone or anything into a God. That includes your mother, and it includes you. Jesus paid for that sin, and now it is finished. It's over.

J: I feel like a thousand-pound weight has been taken off my shoulders.

P: It has been taken away, but it was done two thousand years ago. Your God hasn't given up on you. He never did, and he never will. Jesus did a better job of paying for sin than anyone else ever could, especially would-be gods like you or me. His work finished the job once and for all. Our problems arise when we try to help him do the job he already did perfectly. It just doesn't work, no matter how miserable you make yourself in trying to do it.

J: Do you mean you have tried to do God's job for him too?

P: Everyone has, but now we can keep reminding each other that it doesn't work. He doesn't want us trying to do his job. This time I had the opportunity to remind you. The time will probably come when you'll have to remind me, too.

Consequences of depression can be dramatic. Depression demands a tremendous amount of energy, as people try to do work that human beings are not capable of doing. God's work must be and remain God's work, or the weight we carry will be too heavy for us to bear. That spiritual weight is depression or at least contributes

God's work must be and remain God's work, or the weight we carry will be too heavy for us to bear.

significantly to it. Only when we realize that can we begin to understand the blessings of a spiritual cure in Jesus Christ. So we see that depression often has spiritual roots and spiritual consequences.

CHAPTER FIVE

Spiritual Answers to a Spiritual Problem

As an emotional or mental disorder, depression can be slight or severe. When it is relatively mild, counseling with a Christian counselor or even perhaps a friend will often help to alleviate it. When depression is severe, it usually interrupts a person's life and causes grievous disability. It can be dangerous because it so deeply affects a person's life. Severely depressed people are often unable to perform the simplest tasks of caring for themselves and their families. Severely depressed people may even be suicidal, as we have seen.

In such cases of severe depression, competent psychological and/or psychiatric intervention is essential. Hospitalization is frequently necessary for the severely depressed. Hospitalization will allow professionals to provide more thorough care for them, allow the medical staff to find the proper medication and dosages that may be necessary, and serve to protect the depressed person with competent intervention if suicide is a danger.

Those treatments for depression are important, nonspiritual supports. The Christian, however, will also draw on the spiritual help available. A Christian friend or counselor, a Christian psychologist or pastor, will address the spiritual aspects of depression. They will speak of God's will and way to the one suffering depression and to other members of the family who also need spiritual care. Depression can take a serious toll not only on a person who is depressed, but also on those who must live with the depressed person and are trying to help.

Where is God when I need him?

John has been depressed since he lost his job six months ago. His reaction at first was a normal grief reaction. He did the things you would expect him to do. He didn't want to get up in the morning. He felt worthless and unprofitable. He was concerned about how he would support his family. Then his wife was offered a good job, which she accepted. The income was not quite as much as what John had been making, but the family was doing reasonably well. They were able to do most of the things they had always been able to do.

As time went on, John saw no need to find a job. He already felt worthless. His wife's ability to earn a living independently only made matters worse. John felt like an unnecessary burden on the family. He refused to eat because he didn't believe he had a right to use up the family's food. He would seldom get out of bed during the day because he found no reason to get up and do nothing when everyone else was busy all day long. More and more frequently he experienced a desire to kill himself so he wouldn't be such a burden on everyone else.

John really wanted everyone to be helplessly dependent on him, but they weren't.

Eventually John did attempt suicide. He got up enough energy to go out to the closed garage and start the car. He sat in it until he passed out. Fortunately the car was low on fuel and the engine died before John did. When his children found him and called for emergency service, John was angry that he didn't die. His anger with the family, especially with his wife, came to the surface. John really wanted everyone to be helplessly dependent on him, but they weren't. Everything went along quite well in spite of John's inability to find a job and earn the family income.

As you consider John's situation here, can you imagine that he might have a reason for asking, "Where is God when I need him?"

Think about John's wife. She was doing the best she could. She thought she was doing the right thing. She was trying to help. Can you imagine her asking, "Where is God when I need him?"

What about John's children? They came home from school to find their father close to death in the family car. They had to take the responsibility of providing emergency service to save their father's life. Besides that, they had to try to understand why their father would do such a thing to himself. Finally, they were faced with the horrible prospect of losing their father and losing him in a way that would have a devastating impact on them and their mother for the rest of their lives. Perhaps you can hear them saying, "Where is God when I need him?"

John's condition required hospitalization for his own protection. He also needed medication for the depression he was experiencing. However, none of that could really heal all the problems he and the family experienced. They all needed God. But where does God fit in? What could God do that medication and professionals in the mental health field couldn't do? God could satisfy the spiritual needs of these people. Let's see what those needs were.

It's all my problem

Perhaps by now you have recognized the common thread that is running through this case study. In every case, each person is likely to think that everything is all his or her problem. John thinks the problem is all centered around him. John's wife thinks she should be able to hold the family together and get John out of his depression. The children are almost victims of the circumstance, facing some of the black sides of life that they neither know how to deal with nor even understand. Let's see what kind of spiritual needs and spiritual help can be provided for each of these persons.

The most obvious place to start is with John himself. When he lost his job, he sustained a serious shock to his system. He depended on his job security. He had a difficult time finding anything good in his situation. He could hardly imagine God allowing it to happen. He was cast adrift.

We can learn from John's setback that security is not to be found with human beings. Security found in human beings, whether they are family, employers, friends, or doctors, is a false security. As God has warned: "Cursed is the one who trusts in man . . . and whose heart turns away from the LORD" (Jeremiah 17:5). God wants us to look first to him for security. "Blessed is the man who trusts in the LORD, whose confidence is in him" (Jeremiah 17:7).

Security found in human beings, whether they are family, employers, friends, or doctors, is a false security.

John was trusting his employers to keep him in a job that would allow him to provide for his family. As with many of us, it had never occurred to him that he could lose that security. And he could not cope when it happened.

In connection with the ensuing depression, John had the spiritual need to learn that he could not find security apart from God. That was where he needed to grow spiritually. John's situation forced him to learn that God requires and deserves first place in his life. God should have been in first place all along. John was also learning that God is worthy of trust. God would not let him down.

John had other problems that deserve consideration. He began to think of himself as worthless because he was no longer providing the income for the family. He naturally viewed himself as the breadwinner for the family. The problem was that his role as breadwinner was the measure that determined his value to the family and his own personal value. Since he was not providing the income and since the income was his measure for personal value, he concluded, irrationally, that he was worth nothing because his income was nothing.

His thinking completely ignored that people are not valuable because of what they have or what they do. People are valuable because God decided we are valuable. God not only made us and gave us life, he graciously determined that John and all other human beings were worth the sacrifice of his own Son's life. John needed to understand that God did that, and more important, God did that for him. Even though he was worthless in his own eyes, he was precious in God's eyes.

To put it another way, John may be as worthless as he thinks he is. No one is arguing whether John is doing enough to be a valuable person. Maybe he isn't accomplishing enough to be valuable to anyone. That doesn't matter. The essential fact that no one can argue is that God sent his Son Jesus to sacrifice his life so John could be one of God's people. God decided to do that based only on his immeasurable love. God, for his own sake, valued the otherwise worthless John.

People are valuable because God decided we are valuable.

By feeling so worthless and ignoring God, John in reality has exalted himself, though he obviously doesn't see it that way. You, too, may find it difficult to see anything exalted about John's situation. But consider this. John believes he is worthless, but God says he isn't. John thinks God has abandoned him, but God says he loves John. Whom has John put in first place? Himself—over God! He has placed his own feelings and values above God's. John needs to learn in a patient and loving presentation of both law and gospel that he has no basis or right to make such a judgment. If he believes one thing and God says another, then John must listen to God.

In simple terms, the reason God doesn't seem to fit into John's thinking is that John has made himself into his own god. He believes what he thinks instead of believing what God has said. Ignoring God's authority, he has made himself into an authority on the subject of his own value and worth. That responsibility is too big for a human being to carry. It's no wonder John doesn't have the incentive or energy to do anything. He is worn out from trying to do God's work. The important lesson for John to learn is that he is destroying himself trying to do what God has already done for him, namely, make himself worthy.

Even though he was worthless in his own eyes, he was precious in God's eyes.

Having touched on John's spiritual problems in the midst of his depression, what about the other members of the family? Keep in mind, as we have noted, that spiritually, depression often leaves a person noticeably self-centered. You have already seen some of that self-centeredness in John's thinking. The other members of the family were affected in a similar way.

Think of John's wife, Diane. Diane did the natural thing when John lost his job and didn't see any hope for finding another one in the near future. Diane went to work earning the necessary income to get the family through those difficult times. In the meantime, John was home doing nothing.

It was only a matter of time before Diane started to resent John's apparent laziness. She didn't want to come home at night and see him miserable. She didn't want to feel guilty because she was working and he wasn't. Should she express her anger to motivate John? Should she quit her job so John could know he was needed? What would she do if he attempted suicide again? What about all the hospital bills left after the last attempt?

Diane is in what we might call an "I should be able to fix this" mode. She isn't doing or thinking anything that is wrong in and of itself. The real problem lies in thinking that she has to do it all alone. God's promise that he will never leave her nor forsake her (cf. Deuteronomy 31:6) is far back in her thinking, at best.

The real problem lies in thinking that she has to do it all alone.

We can predict the results. She will carry the burden of trying to alleviate John's condition. She will feel responsible for causing it and for removing it. This will place her under considerable stress that will probably show in frequent outbursts of anger and severe inner tension. In addition to that, she will probably not think along God-pleasing lines when deciding how to handle the problem. Rather than telling John things that he needs to hear, she will probably not say anything at all, or she will say things that will protect herself and the other members of the family.

We might wonder, "What else could she do?" "What would I do?" Christians often find themselves in a position of wondering what is the loving thing to do. We think about it. We pray about it. We also need to learn what God's Word tells us about it. The Scriptures will show us the true and self-sacrificing kind of love to show.

First, John needs to know that he is breaking the First Commandment: "You shall have no other gods before me" (Exodus 20:3). God would want John to know that he was placing his own thoughts and values above God's. At the very least, John needs to know that he is contributing to his own problem.

John, however, probably will not be too happy to hear that. He might rebel at the thought. It won't be easy for Diane to confront John about his sin. Because it isn't easy, Diane may feel that confrontation is the wrong thing to do, and we might agree. We might decide it is more important to protect ourselves from some kind of counterattack than to benefit the depressed person. Self-preservation might become the dominant motivating force.

At the very least, John needs to know that he is contributing to his own problem.

When we feel that way, we need to remember Jesus' self-sacrificing love and the service he asked of his disciples on the night he was betrayed: "You should do as I have done for you" (John 13:15). Jesus always thought of the will of his Father and the welfare of the world he came to save, even though it cost him his life. That is not only the model, it is also the motive for deciding how we will show love. Jesus showed love in actions that were always directed to the benefit of others according to the will of his Father. He acted for others, not himself. In love, he paid the price so others would not have to pay it.

Diane, then, needs to hear that God expects her to be a messenger for John. God does not expect her to do what he alone can do. Diane's problem stretches beyond her ability to reach. She needs God's help, but she does not need just a few Scripture passages to think about. She needs the truth of the law to see her own limitations. She needs the gospel to see the facts that verify God's promises of faithful love and support. That way she herself can become a messenger for God instead of attempting to do God's work for him.

Finally, what about the spiritual needs of the children? They feel guilty because they wonder if they might not be contributing to the problems their father is having. After all, if he didn't have to support them, money wouldn't be such a problem. Since they require care and support, everything would be better if they weren't there. Their feelings of guilt also involve the same kind of helpless feelings their mother is experiencing. They may need counseling, and they surely can use some Christian support. Fellow Christians can address some of the children's doubts and fears in the light of God's truth.

Jesus always thought of the will of his Father and the welfare of the world he came to save, even though it cost him his life.

In their situation, the children are ripe to learn more about their dependence on God and their worth in God's sight. Even though children have every right to expect their parents to take care of them, they, and all of us, need to understand human limitations. Sometimes people face problems such as John faced. Sometimes, for one reason or another, parents are unable to fulfill their parental responsibilities.

For that reason, we must consistently teach the scriptural truth that parents, children, and all people are in the hands of God who takes care of everything. We may not like the way he does it, but his ways are right. We may not understand what he is doing, but he is God. We may do the best we can from day to day, but we are still sinners who make mistakes, who have limitations, who forget to turn to God constantly. In short, Jesus meant it when he said, "Apart from me you can do nothing" (John 15:5).

You never outgrow your need for God

We have given you some different ways of thinking about God's involvement in depression or in the lives of those who live with depressed people. We want to help you think in terms of God's relationship with depressed people and their families. Since depressed people are so likely to limit their thinking to themselves, particularly their own weaknesses and failures, we must be prepared to help them think beyond self to God, for his unique help. These attempts will likely meet with resistance, but we cannot allow that to deter us from patiently pointing a person to God. We need to do so in the spirit of God's law and gospel. The law shows us our limitations. The gospel shows that God's love and power in Christ is unlimited.

> Since a depressed person is so likely to limit his thinking to himself, we must be prepared to help him or her think beyond self to God, for his unique help.

The Christian message is that God's great love for the world moved him to send his own Son, Jesus Christ, to live in perfection for us. In his love, Jesus sacrificed his life for the sins of the world. In his love and power, Jesus rose to live and rule eternally. These are historical facts. These facts of our salvation are true whether we believe them or not. They are objective truths based on God's grace and his work to reconcile the world to himself in Christ.

The Christian message counters depression's tendencies. Depression focuses inwardly; God's Word and work focus outwardly toward God. God's Word and work turn attention away from the individual to God. Spiritually, we all need God-focus, and we may, therefore, need therapy that will address the problem of self-focus that is intensified with depression. God is the object of all real hope. We need to offer that hope.

Depression focuses inwardly; God's Word and work focus outwardly toward God.

Keeping God and his good news in the picture is essential. Any person who looks within himself will always find justifiable reason to be depressed. For the depressed, looking within himself will only provide more evidence, then, that depression is justifiable and the cure hopeless.

Let us, therefore, review the objective truths we Christians know that focus on God. As you read through them, think of new ways you can apply them to the depression you are facing. Think of what is happening to you. Then, imagine that God is talking directly to you (he is!) with his truth. Think about what that means for you. God knows what you are facing. He has the answer.

The First Commandment

Every sin at its root is a sin against the First Commandment. Any sin against any of God's commandments always puts us in the position of deciding that we know better than God does. In a sense, every sin against any commandment amounts to saying, "I want to be god, and I am going to be my own god instead of letting God be God." Whenever that happens, you can expect serious consequences.

When an individual places the responsibility on himself for being unerringly correct, infallible in his judgments, and solely responsible for doing superhuman work, the toll will be great. You can expect emotional and physical consequences like those related to depression.

It's been said that every sin, in its essence, is an attempt to dethrone God. Sin began for humanity with Adam and Eve trying to dethrone God at Satan's prompting in the Garden of Eden. As then, so now, we can expect problems when we try to make little gods out of ourselves. For example, if you try to do God's work in fighting to cure depression by yourself, you can expect that you will be carrying a weight that is too great for a human being to carry. Only God is almighty and all-knowing—unlimited in his abilities and unfailing in making the correct choices. When individuals place the responsibility on themselves for being unerringly correct, infallible in their judgments, and solely responsible for doing superhuman work, the toll will be great. You can expect emotional and physical consequences like those related to depression.

The sin against the first commandment will naturally place you in opposition to God. That is a no-win situation. Either you can expect to reap the results of what you sow for yourself, or God will actively frustrate your efforts. If you try to use your own efforts, apart from God, to cure your depression or to help someone else eliminate theirs, your frustrations and frailties will probably become obvious in a short time.

That is the time to examine yourself to find out whether you have ignored God and his love and strength. Those frustrations and frailties may be God's way of letting you know you're trying to get along without him. When you realize that danger, you might even thank God for the frustration and pain because God is teaching you how much you need him as God. Then, the important step to take is to repent of your sin.

The righteousness of Christ

The righteousness of Christ was a phrase that frightened Martin Luther in his early life. He thought the righteousness of Christ was something Christ demanded of him, something he had to earn by his efforts at keeping God's law. When Luther learned from Romans 1:16,17 ("a righteousness from God . . . that is by faith") and other passages that the righteousness of Christ is God's gift, that it is good news and not bad news, he found the key to God's love. The good news is that Jesus kept God's law and he gives us the credit for his work. That is the righteousness of Christ, righteousness God counts for us.

That good news brings needed, longed-for comfort to people who are depressed. The depressed are usually extra hard on themselves, seeing only their bad qualities. Those qualities may or may not be as bad as a depressed person thinks they are. It is a marvel of God's love, therefore, to learn, regardless of how you feel, that God counts Christ's righteousness as yours. It is a wonderful privilege too to be able to tell others, regardless of how they feel, that God judges them on Christ's merits rather than their own.

Again, to put it another way, God is not impressed by what you have done, nor is he frustrated by your failures. God makes his judgment on the basis of Jesus' record. That record is perfect. The Christian is perfect in God's sight because Jesus is perfect. That is what the righteousness of Christ means.

Christ's work of redemption

Christ's work of redemption is another phrase that often confuses or mystifies people. In reality it is simple and clear and the heart and core of our Christianity. All Christians, depressed or not, can always benefit from hearing more of redemption.

Right there on the cross, when Jesus died, all those sins were paid for.

The word *redemption* has to do with paying a debt. Christ paid our debt for sins when he sacrificed his own life on the cross. God says in his law: "You must pay for not keeping me first in your life." But then God says in his gospel of redemption: "Christ paid your debt for you when he died. You are redeemed."

Now, once the law makes a particular sin clear, the gospel invites the sinner on the most important spiritual journey any person can make. That journey is a trip to the cross of Jesus Christ. Think of John once again from our case study. He is burdened with his own depression, frightened, and virtually paralyzed. Now let's envision helping John make his own personal trip to the cross. There John would be able to say:

> Lord Jesus, I have put more value on the money I was able to earn than on my own value in your eyes. I thought I was worthless, and you proved that I was

worth your life. I am sorry for thinking that my values were correct and yours were wrong. I am sorry I have been so ungrateful for the gifts you have given me to earn a living. I am sorry I have tried to give myself the position of god in my own life. That position only belongs to you. Forgive me for my misdirected thinking.

Jesus' answer to that confession was spoken from the cross itself. He said, "It is finished" (John 19:30). Right there on the cross, when Jesus died, all those sins were paid for.

Diane needs to take a similar trip. While there, she might say:

Lord Jesus, I have been working so hard trying to handle all these problems alone that I have forgotten about you and your almighty power and faithful love. Forgive me for trying to do your job. You are almighty. I am not. You know all the right answers. I don't. Forgive me for my feeble and mistaken efforts.

Once again the answer of Jesus, already supported by his death on the cross, is, "It is finished. I have forgiven you, Diane. Your sins have all been paid for."

Do you see how personal Jesus' message is?

Imagine going to the cross with John and Diane's children. They might be led to confess that they were depending so much on their parents to take care of everything that they forgot God. They, too, need the peace and assurance Jesus gives. Jesus' answer is still the same. "It is finished. Welcome to a brand new understanding of my love."

Christ's work of redemption is not mysterious, and it is not confusing. It is free and complete. But we don't want to get the idea that because forgiveness is full and free it was won without cost. Free means someone else paid. Anything that is free to you had to be paid for by someone else. Your forgiveness was paid for by Jesus Christ.

Christ has invited you to come to his cross. Bring any sin on your mind and heart, and have Jesus show you personally the way he paid for that sin. Think then of the prices that John, Diane, and their children were willing to pay of themselves to try to find peace in their family. Those attempts only kept them from recognizing the work Jesus already did for them. They needed that trip to the cross.

A true Christian friend

Sometimes we need someone to help or we need to be helpers to get Jesus and his cross in focus. That's when Christian friendship can shine.

Christ has invited you to come to his cross. Bring any sin on your mind and heart, and have Jesus show you personally the way he paid for that sin.

A Christian friend may come in all sorts of forms. A friend may be your spouse or another family member or just a close friend. Your best Christian friend may be your pastor. Perhaps that special friend is a counselor or a Christian psychologist. The best friend that you can have, regardless of the position that person holds in your life, is the friend who will speak God's law when you need to hear it so that he or she can also present God's gospel directly to your guilt, your anger, your misdirected thinking. The best friends you have are the friends who tell you what you need to hear, not what you want to hear. More than anything else, your friend will be a messenger of God.

Perhaps the example of John, Diane, and family has helped you to realize that even Christians who know the truth of God's Word are often unable to apply it to themselves as they need to in troubled times. Perhaps you have realized by now that depressed people are among the least likely to be able to make these applications themselves. The whole nature of depression is to look inward when you need to be looking outward. If you are depressed, at the very least, seek a spiritual guide, a Christian friend, who will direct you to the truth of God's law and gospel. If you are helping someone who is depressed, be sure to include the law and gospel as essential for lasting relief.

Professional assistance for depression is often important in the healing process, even as it is in medical emergencies. At the same time, as with surgery for example, spiritual concerns have a top priority. Most Christians would like to have their pastor bring them the Word of God when they are hospitalized. That means most Christians recognize the need for the Word of God even at times when many other professionals in the secular field are also working on their behalf. It should be no different when depression strikes. God remains the Great Physician both of soul and body.

The best friends you have are the friends who tell you what you need to hear, not what you want to hear.

Yes, the depressed person still needs God as much as anyone else. It is possible, however, that a depressed person may not recognize that need. As a Christian friend, you may be able to help a depressed person see the need for God. God provides all the unlimited blessings of healing and spiritual growth. With God, we can learn to live with depression, if necessary. Anyone would be better off living with depression than living without God.

Thank God for my depression

No one who is depressed would be able to understand thanking God or anyone else for a depression. Only when God's healing takes place will a person realize that God can use a horrible experience to produce a blessed result. He used the horror of the cross of Jesus to accomplish the salvation of the world. That illustrates dramatically and verifies the promise: "And we know that in all things God works for the good of those who love him" (Romans 8:28). Now look further in that same passage, and see why God works so much good for us. He does so for "those . . . who have been called according to his purpose." God's purpose is your salvation that only Jesus could accomplish. Jesus' work is done. God will be at work throughout your lifetime to help you understand that more clearly. If he uses a depression to help teach you, thank God for your depression.

CHAPTER SIX

How Do You Help a Depressed Person? ~~~~~~~~~~~~~~

We have examined the disorder known as depression. We have considered physical causes, emotional causes, and spiritual causes, realizing that the cause may also be a combination of any of these. We have described various means for the treatment of depression and ways to get help for depression.

Sometimes, at least when the depression is not severe, you yourself can look for the help that you need. However, just because depression "presses down," you may often find yourself helpless to do anything. More often, someone else must take the initiative to help.

So, what if you are that someone else and in the position of helping someone who is depressed? How do you know what to do? For that matter, how do you keep yourself from becoming depressed while dealing with the problem? You may wonder whether you should be calling your doctor or your pastor. You may not know a competent counselor, psychologist, or psychiatrist. You may not know the difference between a psychologist and a psychiatrist. You may be thinking about the stigma that some people still attach to mental illnesses and emotional disorders. As a helper, you may wonder where to find a Christian psychologist or psychiatrist who will reinforce the faith that you and your loved one have.

To make matters more difficult, it's hard to know when to take action. Depressions may develop so slowly that it becomes difficult to see how bad things are getting. If you are close to a depressed person, you will probably get accustomed to a loved one—whether spouse, child, or parent—being "down."

In other instances, however, particularly if an attempted suicide is involved, you will know the depression demands immediate attention. But then where do you go? What hospitals have the facilities for treating depression? Our society is generally better equipped to deal with clear medical emergencies than with emotional or mental emergencies. You can call 911 or whatever your local emergency number is, and people will take care of the sick or injured person. Generally speaking, though, people are not as well equipped to deal with emergencies that stem from mental and emotional problems. This chapter will guide you as you seek to help someone who is depressed.

THE RESOURCES AVAILABLE

The resources for helping depressed individuals are many and varied. For our purposes, we will consider individual and institutional resources for help.

Individual resources begin with you.

Individual resources

Individual resources begin with you. Don't underestimate your own ability to be a resource for a depressed person. You are probably closer to that person than anyone else. Usually a spouse is the first to recognize a depression. Regardless of who the depressed member of the family is, however, family members are more likely to see depression than those outside the family. All of us have seen examples of people laughing on the outside while crying on the inside. Family members are the most likely to see what is going on inside.

Recognizing a depression is the beginning of healing.

You may find that your wife, "Linda," seems sad most of the time. She seems to cry at the drop of the hat. She doesn't speak openly the way she used to. You don't know of problems between you, but something isn't right. You're not experiencing tension in the family as much as you feel a cloud over everything. Could Linda be depressed? Is there something you can do? You ask if something is wrong and the answer keeps coming back, "No, nothing." Don't give up trying to talk. Don't assume everything is fine.

One way to determine what is causing a depression is to try to establish when it began. What else was going on in Linda's life at the time? Did the children leave for school? Is the youngest just entering school? Did Linda have to leave work? Did she have to start work after years of being at home? Did a relative die? Rather than trying to figure out for yourself what must be going on, it's better to ask questions. Thinking the way a depressed person thinks is not an easy task. Let him or her do the talking. Questions about when the depression started are often good ways of getting conversation and open discussion started.

One way to determine what is causing a depression is to try to establish when it began.

Remember that depressed people are extremely busy using a great deal of energy thinking about themselves and their own problems. When you try to tell them what you think is going on in their minds and what they should be doing about it, they will most likely resist your thoughts and suggestions. They know more about their problems than you do.

Linda, for example, is more likely to respond favorably to gentle hints and encouragement than to "Just do this. Just do that. You shouldn't be thinking that way." Instead, "I don't know what is wrong, but I want you to know I'm still here and I still care. Please talk to me and help me understand" will usually be received much better.

Remember that depressed people are extremely busy using a great deal of energy thinking about themselves and their own problems.

By now you can see how you must exercise much patience in dealing with a depressed person. Being with someone who is depressed can be depressing. It's important to continue to be patient and to be ready to ask forgiveness from God and the depressed person when you're not understanding the depression. You may have to ask Linda to come with you to the cross of your Savior to lay down the sins both of you have committed and leave them there. Jesus will reassure both of you of his forgiveness. Equipped with his forgiveness, you will gain strength to forgive one another.

As a Christian, never forget the power of prayer in your life. Helping a depressed person can be frustrating. You may sometimes feel responsible for making your depressed loved one better. But no one can make someone else better; all we can do is to help and guide healing. You will find great peace of mind, then, by going to your Savior with the simple admission:

"I can't make him or her happy. I can't make the depression go away."

The loving and almighty Savior's response is, "I know you can't. Put the problem on me and let me handle it in the way I know is best" (cf. 1 Peter 5:7: "Cast all your anxiety on him because he cares for you"). The comfort and power of prayer is not only for depressed people, it is for you, too, as you help a depressed person.

This also brings up another important consideration. One psychologist put it this way: "After I have dealt for several sessions with a person who doesn't seem to be responding to treatment, I begin to suspect that this person just wants to be depressed. People are sympathetic with depressed people, at least early in the depression. Sometimes depressed people get what they want by being depressed.

It's important to continue to be patient and to be ready to ask forgiveness from God and the depressed person when you're not understanding the depression.

Getting what you want, whether it's attention or something else, can be a good reason for being depressed. After a few sessions like that, I will often ask a depressed person how long he or she wants to be depressed."

This psychologist was noting that some people are depressed because they choose to be depressed. Several writers in the field of psychology in general and depression in particular strongly emphasize the part that personal decision and choice play in depression. Some, like Dr. William Glasser, founder of the Institute for Reality Therapy and author of several books, including *Reality Therapy* and *Control Theory*, go so far as to say that people choose depression as their personal way of reacting to an event as severe as the loss of a loved one. In his words, "They depress."

Sometimes depressed people get what they want by being depressed.

When it comes to deciding whether a person is a victim of or is choosing depression, you probably will not feel competent to judge. Very likely you should look for a more objective opinion.

For us as Christians, **the next natural resource is the pastor.** Within our circles, pastors have a wide spectrum of abilities in counseling. Some are highly qualified and enjoy any opportunity to provide counseling services to their parishioners. Some have had the opportunity to add specialized training in counseling to their theological training. Still others, just as faithful in their service to the Lord and his Church, do not have special interest or ability in this area.

In spite of this diversity of interest and ability, all faithful pastors have the most important equipment of all, the Word of God. The Word of God has support and encouragement for you as well as for the person you seek to help. The promise of Christ, "I am with you always, to the very end of the age" (Matthew 28:20), offers comfort for you, the depressed, and every other Christian.

We have already discussed a variety of ways both the law and gospel can be used. Your pastor can give you more personal and direct advice on how you can use it yourself. He can assist you to find the Word of God that applies to you or the one you are trying to help. Perhaps you and your pastor can talk to the depressed person together. His purpose will be to share the Word of God, to confront with God's law in preparation for sharing the sweet and healing news of the gospel. He will not or should not attempt to do psychological work above and beyond his capabilities, nor should you expect him to do that. The pastor is first a healer of souls, with the Word of God as his tool.

The Word of God remains the constant in pastoral counseling. Genuine Christian or pastoral counseling always includes Christ. In addition, the pastor is still more likely than most people outside the mental health field to have the objective ability to recognize the problem of depression. Since depression and other disorders are more common than most of us would think, the pastor has likely seen these disorders before. He might provide a good first avenue for assisting you to determine how severe the problem is.

Genuine Christian or pastoral counseling always includes Christ.

In most cases, whether the pastor is only one step toward healing in depression or whether he is all the farther you need to go in mild cases of depression, the pastor should be there for you. You should seek his continuing support to provide for your own spiritual needs as well as the depressed person's. However, other steps may be necessary.

This may be a good time to establish a rule for yourself and anyone else involved in the healing process in depression. That rule is: **when in doubt, overtreat.** The rule bears repeating and more explanation, which it will receive as we go on.

A Christian counselor may be the next person for you to contact. Your pastor may feel that this depression seems to be particularly severe. He may wish to direct you to other professional assistance. He may refer you to a trusted Christian counselor or to an agency like The Wisconsin Lutheran Child and Family Service (WLCFS) where licensed and skilled counselors are available to provide further determination of how severe the depression is. These Christian counselors are highly trained both in diagnosis and treatment of disorders like depression. In

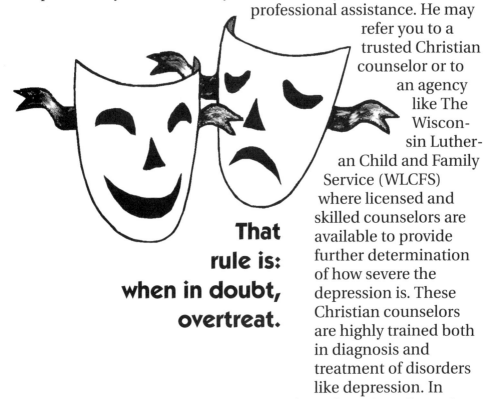

That rule is: when in doubt, overtreat.

addition, they have a referral network in place that allows them to follow our rule easily and directly: **when in doubt, overtreat.**

Most important, church agencies like WLCFS have both the expertise to diagnose, treat, and refer clients who seek help, and the commitment to the Word of God. Counselors are skilled in using the law and gospel. That can assure you that faith in Christ will remain central in the therapeutic process. Usually these trained and committed counselors will work together with the individual's pastor if confidentiality allows and if spiritual assistance seems valuable.

In more severe cases of depression, **a psychologist** should probably be the next level of referral. In most cases, trained counselors hold staff meetings with psychologists to review cases and the progress that is being made. A psychologist will provide important evaluation and advice to counselors as they proceed with their work.

Psychologist usually hold a Ph.D. in the field of psychology. Sometimes they specialize in certain areas within that field, such as education, children, adults, the elderly, or the clinical setting. Psychologists are highly trained and licensed to practice. They will often maintain their own personal practices, while serving as consultants to others. Psychologists may serve on the staffs of one or more hospitals and would likely have the authority to admit a person to a hospital if they determined a need for hospitalization.

The psychologist is highly trained and licensed to practice.

The psychologists' main tool is psychotherapy, sometimes called "talk therapy." The cognitive therapy, the behavior therapy, and the psychodynamic therapy defined at the end of chapter three are examples of "talk therapy." By means of their intense training in abnormal psychology and accepted psychotherapeutic practices, they are qualified to lead a person through a healing (therapeutic) process. Still, psychologists will abide by the same rule we have been repeating for ourselves: **when in doubt, overtreat.**

The psychologist's next step would be **the psychiatrist,** who, in addition to training in psychology, is a medical doctor. While psychiatrists, too, will likely use "talk therapy," they might also use medication that psychologists are not licensed to prescribe. Some psychiatrists are more inclined to use psychotherapy with their patients; some are more inclined to use medication. The psychiatrist has that choice.

In many cases, medication is needed because it is the treatment of choice over psychotherapy. In other cases medication may be used to control the "emotional storm" in the troubled person's mind. To put it another way, in depression or other mental and emotional illnesses, the disturbances in the person's brain can be so severe that they do not allow a person to think clearly. If that person can't think clearly, talking through a problem is not only difficult, but in some cases impossible.

Institutional resources

Even with all the individual resources at our disposal, namely, you, your pastor, a counselor, a psychologist, and a psychiatrist, we may reach the point where the depressed person needs to be institutionalized. Many general hospitals have units for treating mental illness. Often these facilities are locked for the protection of the patients. Visiting hours are usually more strict than in other parts of the hospital. This allows the staff ample time to work with groups of patients and individuals. Check with the hospitals in your area to see whether they maintain such a unit. Most hospitals will be able to handle psychiatric emergencies, but many may refer to other facilities for further treatment.

Many general hospitals have units for treating mental illness.

In addition to local general hospitals, virtually all areas of our country have mental hospitals. These facilities may be private, they may be military veteran facilities, or they may be state owned and operated. These facilities provide the most intense form of treatment.

From a layman's point of view, there are two main reasons for institutionalizing an individual: First, he or she is a danger to self or others. Second, he or she needs close medical observation and evaluation so that drugs can be used. The drug use must be carefully monitored, and often other physical tests are necessary to treat the entire problem. Often the same psychologists and psychiatrists the person met with before will also treat him or her in the hospital.

In most cases, hospitalization is short-term, measured in weeks or perhaps months, but seldom years. In years past, confinement to a mental institution was often a lifetime matter. The treatment of mental disorders has advanced significantly in recent years. In many respects, it is a very young

There are two main reasons for institutionalizing an individual: First, he or she is a danger to self or others. Second, he or she needs close medical observation and evaluation so that drugs can be used.

field, tracing its history only as far back as the forties and fifties. Advancements in the understanding of the brain and its working, advancements in the use of medication, and advancement in various psychotherapies make treatment of depression and other mental disorders much more encouraging than in years gone by. Progress in the field continues to be made rapidly.

As a society, however, we are perhaps advancing more slowly in removing our suspicions and our preconceived notions of hospitals for the mentally ill and our notions about the mentally ill themselves. Many people still feel a stigma attached to mental illness. It is likely that you and your doctor might have some difficulty convincing a severely depressed person to enter a mental institution. But as time goes on and we recognize how many people suffer with depression and other disorders, it is hoped we will begin to realize that mental illness is no more shameful than physical illness. The shame is in not getting help that is available.

It is hoped we will begin to realize that mental illness is no more shameful than physical illness.

In the hospital setting, it continues to be important to remember God and to have your pastor available to share God's Word. Keep in mind that the depressed person is likely to carry feelings of worthlessness with him.

Take the case of Linda, whom we met before. She might not be assuring herself or anyone else that she is a valuable person. She may feel as if she is more trouble than she is worth. And in a sense that might be true, but it is never true in God's sight. Jesus Christ did not go to the cross for everyone except depressed people or the mentally ill. He went to the cross because of his love for all people no matter what their strengths or weaknesses.

If Linda needs hospitalization, don't forget the pastor, who can bring her God's comfort. Here again, in the hospital setting, it is likely that seeing Linda will be more difficult than entering other parts of the hospital. Schedules in these specialized units are usually closely monitored. Arrangements can usually be made, however, if the hospitalized person makes known his or her desire to see the pastor. As the hospital seeks to maintain the individual's confidentiality, it may be necessary for the hospitalized person to make the first move and contact the pastor. The pastor will not likely be able to visit without that invitation and permission.

Where professional treatment and possible hospitalization are involved, usually finances are a concern. That is with good reason. Professional treatment can be expensive. In some cases, as in the example of WLCFS, payment is made on a sliding scale depending on the ability to pay. The remainder of the cost is absorbed by donations and the support of other Christians. On the other hand, psychologists usually have a set fee that may vary from $75 to $150 an hour. It may be more or less, depending on the situation. Few people can afford extended treatment on these terms. Psychiatrists, as medical doctors, are even more expensive. Fees may exceed $100 for a half hour or even fifteen minutes.

Fortunately, now insurance covers most forms of therapy. The reason for licensing in various states is that the license qualifies the person or the agency to bill insurance companies for its services. You should examine your own insurance to see what coverage is allowed and what kinds of treatments are available to you. As in all areas of medical insurance, coverage will vary greatly.

State institutions would be a last resort for those who have no other means of paying for services. That is not to say that these institutions are not valuable and qualified places for providing service. Far from it. Rather, the state institution would naturally expect you to exhaust all other possibilities before it provides these services for you.

You can also expect that the state institution will work diligently to discharge a patient as soon as it is safe to do so. Medication will likely be the avenue of choice for helping the individual. Medication generally works faster to obtain desired results than psychotherapy. Medication by itself, however, is more likely to treat the symptoms than the cause of the depression unless the cause is purely physical. Overcrowding and expense to the state are always underlying considerations.

What I should look for to decide whether treatment is necessary

By now you should realize that you alone don't have to make the decision about what is required for proper treatment. You have many options and resources at your disposal. You are not alone in dealing with a depressed person, and the depressed person you help is not the only depressed person in your town, state, or country. You have resources. You have a channel to follow. You need to be sure of the signals that say something needs to be done.

Physical signals are your first clue. If you see changes in weight, changes in sleep habits, changes in work habits, changes in the way that person acts around you or the other members of the family, it's time to look for help.

The natural place to start when you see changes that are purely physical is with your medical doctor. He or she will be able to examine your loved one and determine whether a physical problem exists. Many physical ailments have symptoms that are similar to symptoms of depression. Many can be treated with medication. For example, a thyroid that is not functioning properly can produce symptoms that seem like a depression to the uninformed. A medical doctor would have to make that diagnosis. Changes in body chemistry can produce similar symptoms, perhaps during a woman's menstrual cycle or menopause. If you see physical symptoms, encourage the person to see a medical doctor as soon as possible. It may take a load off his or her mind and yours too.

> Tom feels worthless these days, and he didn't feel that way before. He cries for no reason. He doesn't like himself and doesn't want to be with other people. He used to wait eagerly for Friday night when a few couples got together, but now he doesn't even want to go. As soon as he gets home, he's up in bed watching television that he doesn't care about. He's not interested in anything.

Emotional signals include such things as a constant feeling of being down, carrying the world on your shoulders.

It's time to seek help for Tom. Things aren't right. You can trust your instincts about that. Getting Tom to talk to a counselor or a psychologist may not be easy. Talking to him yourself may be a strain. Remember to be patient at the same time as you need to be firm. If he doesn't want to get help for his own sake, help him at least to think about what is happening to the family around him because of this problem. Maybe it's a depression and maybe it's not. You don't have to be an expert on the subject; you only need to point him to someone who is. Offer to go along. Just be there.

You don't have to be an expert on the subject; you only need to point him to someone who is.

Ann used to go to church every Sunday, and home devotions were always a part of her life as long as Larry, her husband, could remember. But that's all changed now. She doesn't want to have anything to do with the church or the Word. Everyone else in the church is always looking at her, or worse, looking down on her. They have everything so good, and she has never felt so bad.

Spiritual signals include feelings of guilt and worthlessness. As we have seen, alienation from God and other people is often part of a depression.

The natural place to start is with the pastor of your church. Again it is unlikely that Ann will want to go right away. The pastor is a spokesman for God, and remember how Ann feels about God right now. The same kind of patient forcefulness is still important. If she won't go alone, go yourself or invite the pastor to stop and see Ann. It may be some time before she is willing to listen to what he has to say, and she might not be an enthusiastic counselee, but don't rule out the help before you make an attempt. The help is there.

ALWAYS TAKE A SUICIDE THREAT SERIOUSLY.

A suicide threat is the overriding signal that help is essential. ALWAYS TAKE A SUICIDE THREAT SERIOUSLY.

A suicide threat does not always mean that a person attempts suicide. You will be able to hear indications of suicidal thoughts. "I don't want to live anymore." "I can't go on this way." "You can have my things; I won't need them anymore." "You'll be sorry when I'm gone." These words may or may not be suicide threats, but remember our rule: **when in doubt, overtreat.**

Professionals always take suicide threats seriously, and we all need to learn from them. To illustrate how seriously professionals take this matter, threat of suicide is one of only a few instances when a person can be hospitalized for a limited amount of time against his or her own will.

Under no circumstances should you keep your suspicions of a suicidal condition to yourself. Share them with your pastor. Share them with your medical doctor. Share them with a counselor you have been working with. Just share them. Only five percent of those who attempt suicide succeed, but that is too much of a risk to decide for yourself that your loved one isn't "that bad yet."

In conclusion

You have help available. You have some examples of the kinds of signals that indicate depression in its various stages from mild to severe. Getting your loved one to accept help and treatment may be easy because he or she already feels miserable enough to do something about it. Or, it may be difficult because he or she doesn't have the energy or the desire to do anything about it. You are not alone, and neither is the depressed person you want to help.

Above all, God is in control of everything, from the knowledge he gives to your helpers to the helpers themselves, to the financial considerations, to the support you and your family need yourselves. "He who did not spare his own Son, but gave him up for us all—how will he not also, along with him, graciously give us all things?" (Romans 8:32) God, who gave you his own Son Jesus, will give you what you need now. Use the help God gives.

CHAPTER 7

Bible Studies for Understanding and Dealing with Depression

The Bible offers several examples of people who were depressed. This section is intended to allow you to study some of these examples carefully. As you do, we will lead you to examine possible causes of depression so that you can see whether any of the patterns that become evident apply to you. More important, this will give you an opportunity to see God's involvement with the depressed person. Did God provide answers? Did the answers work? Are there lessons you can learn as you face depression yourself or with someone you care deeply about?

Look for one thing to be consistent in this study. Look for the faithfulness of God in his power and love to bless his people in their suffering. That faithfulness will never change. These people of the Bible and heroes of faith were no more important to God than you are now. We can always pray to God for his help and direction. We need to do that continually. We also need to remember, however, that God speaks to us in his Word. In the midst of depression, it may be a good time to let God do most of the talking.

Elijah—Prophet of God

Elijah was one of God's most faithful servants. He was a type of John the Baptist, who fearlessly preached the Word of God regardless of whether people were willing to listen. Elijah was one along with Moses who appeared with Jesus to the disciples on the Mount of Transfiguration. One would be hard-pressed to find a more faithful and productive servant of God. But now read 1 Kings 19:1-18.

Elijah had called down fire from heaven to consume his sacrifice and prove that the Lord God was the one true God. Four hundred fifty priests of Baal hadn't been able to do that after trying all day long. Elijah won the contest. More exactly, the Lord had won the contest. No one could doubt who was God and who wasn't.

Chapter 19 tells us that Jezebel, the wicked wife of King Ahab, was determined to kill Elijah as soon as she could get her hands on him. It doesn't seem to make sense that Elijah would be afraid of the threat after God had performed such an incredible miracle and won such an incredible battle. Nevertheless, Elijah sounded depressed. He was ready to say that his life had gone on long enough.

1 Kings 19:1-18 (Answer key on pages 107 and 108)

Read verses 1 to 5a

What was at the root of Elijah's fear?

Why was Elijah's fear unfounded?

How did Elijah show that he was in a state of depression?

What are some of the signs of depression that Elijah demonstrated?

What losses might Elijah have been thinking about?

Read verses 5b to 9a

How did God show that he was concerned about Elijah's physical needs?

What have you learned about depression that would indicate that this is a reasonable concern here?

What indications does the Bible give that Elijah's needs went beyond the physical need for food and sleep?

Read verses 9b to 14

How did God address the self-centeredness of Elijah's depression?

What was the significance of the appearance of God to Elijah?

What was the significance of the wind, the earthquake, and the fire that God was not in?

What does the sound of the gentle whisper teach us about God's dealings with Elijah?

What do Elijah's actions in the presence of God show us?

What was God doing by focusing Elijah's attention on himself?

How does Elijah's repeated answer to God make it clear that he still had much to learn?

Read verses 15 to 18

How does God address Elijah's needs in these verses?

What is God aware of that Elijah is not thinking about?

How does God demonstrate his patience with his servant?

What do God's commands to anoint other servants demonstrate to Elijah and us about God's control?

How might this question of who is in control cause Elijah to feel isolated, depressed, and anxious?

King David

The most faithful king in Israel's history was King David, an example for all who followed him. The Bible tells us about many sides of this hero of faith. He was a man of God, but he was also a mere human being. He had human frailties and human weaknesses, both spiritually and physically. His strengths and weaknesses allow us to relate to him and realize that he was much the same as we are. The Bible gives us accounts of real people with whom we can relate when we see the difficulties that confronted them and the troubles they brought upon themselves. David is that kind of real person.

Perhaps the most powerful record of David's faithfulness and trust in God was his battle with Goliath. Then he appeared bigger than life, but a model for a life of trust in God. His greatest spiritual lapse was his adultery with Bathsheba and the subsequent murder of her husband, Uriah. Then he hit the pits, where many of us have had our own sordid experiences.

Following his spiritual crash, David lived for almost a year in a state of impenitence. He lived with his own guilt, unwilling to confess it and find forgiveness for it. Only when David's "pastor," Nathan, confronted David was he ready to confess the guilt of his sin (see 2 Samuel 12:1-14).

In at least two psalms, David speaks of his sin and the accompanying blessing of God's forgiveness. Read 2 Samuel 11 and 12 to see God's record of David's sin and the way God sought to regain this sinner to a state of forgiveness. Read Psalm 32 and Psalm 51 to see how David's sin affected him and more important, how God's forgiveness blessed him. Now let's focus on Psalm 32.

Psalm 32 (Answer key on pages 109 and 110)

Read verses 1 to 2

How does David's experience add meaning to his expression of the blessing of forgiveness in these verses?

How does David appear in these verses to be longing for something he has lost?

How does David describe forgiveness in a way that would comfort a person who is depressed and thinking about his own guilt?

Read verses 3 to 4

What are some of the typical signs of depression in these verses?

What physical suffering does David describe?

How does David describe his emotional suffering?

How does David's physical and emotional suffering relate to his spiritual condition?

Why does this relationship between the physical, emotional, and spiritual exist?

Why was David fertile ground for Satan when he was in this state?

Read verse 5

Why did David finally confess his sins (remember 2 Samuel 12:1-14)?

What does this teach us about the need for a Christian friend or counselor when one is in a state of depression?

What were the benefits of confession?

Why is confession more than a psychological release?

What is the most important part of a Christian's confession of sins?

Read verses 8 to 11

What indications does Scripture provide that David's suffering was over?

What indications does the psalm provide that David truly believed and appreciated God's forgiveness?

What did David's appreciation for God's forgiveness prompt him to do?

How is David a model for us in our concern about others who might be depressed?

The Apostle Paul

Scripture does not indicate that the great Apostle Paul, Missionary to the Gentiles, was ever really depressed. He did have a thorn in the flesh that he prayed God would take from him, and God did not take it away (2 Corinthians 11 to 12). God knew Paul needed that thorn in the flesh to help Paul remain truly dependent on God. That, in simplest terms, is what the Bible means by true humility. Paul learned humility, total dependence on God, through the way God cared for him.

Rather than giving us an example of depression, Paul provides an example of a person who had every human reason to be depressed, but wasn't. The book of Philippians has been called Paul's epistle of joy. Read the four chapters of this little book and look for the joy Paul expresses there. Realize as you read the book that Paul was in prison at the time he wrote it, because he was a believer in and a teacher of Christ. Even though Paul did not expect to die at this time in his life and didn't, Paul knew that the possibility of his being executed was real. After reading the entire epistle, concentrate on chapter 1.

Philippians 1 (Answer key on pages 110-112)

Read verses 3 to 11

How does Paul demonstrate his love and concern for the Philippians?

How does he show that he considers their concerns understandable?

What do the Philippians appear to be overlooking in their concerns for Paul?

How is Paul's concern for the Philippians an indication that Paul was not depressed in his difficult situation?

Read verses 12 to 14

How is God's control evident in Paul's life?

How was God's control able to do more than any human being could accomplish?

How did God keep his promise to make all things work out for the good of Paul and Christ's Church?

Why would understanding this control of God prevent a person from falling into a depression that has spiritual roots?

Read verses 18 to 26

What gave Paul the confidence that God would take care of him in his current situation?

What was the extent of Paul's confidence?

What was Paul's primary concern?

What was the difference between St. Paul's desire to depart and be with the Lord and thoughts of suicide a depressed person might have?

What showed that Paul was willing either to die or to live in contentment?

Answer Keys

1 Kings 19:1-18

Read verses 1 to 5a

What was at the root of Elijah's fear? (**He lost confidence in God.**)

Why was Elijah's fear unfounded? (**God would take care of him.**)

How did Elijah show that he was in a state of depression? (**He withdrew by himself.**)

What are some of the signs of depression that Elijah demonstrated? (**He isolated himself. He expressed feelings of worthlessness. He wished he could die. He apparently cared only to sleep.**)

What losses might Elijah have been thinking about? (**He felt that his life's work was all for nothing.**)

Read verses 5b to 9a

How did God show that he was concerned about Elijah's physical needs? (**He sent an angel and provided food and water for Elijah.**)

What have you learned about depression that would indicate that this is a reasonable concern here? (**Elijah was "feeling down," was "acting different," was "feeling worthless," and was "expressing potentially suicidal thoughts."**)

What indications does the Bible give that Elijah's needs went beyond the physical need for food and sleep? (**The angel had to prompt Elijah to eat and drink.**)

Read verses 9b to 14

How did God address the self-centeredness of Elijah's depression? (**He spoke to Elijah and confronted him with his presence.**)

What was the significance of the appearance of God to Elijah? (**Elijah had to talk about what was depressing him. He had to see that he was wrong to feel abandoned by God.**)

What was the significance of the wind, the earthquake, and the fire, that God was not in? (**Elijah had wanted God to work in spectacular ways according to Elijah's own ideas of God. But God has his own ways.**)

What does the sound of the gentle whisper teach us about God's dealings with Elijah? (**God works in quiet, gentle ways through his Word to reach his people.**)

What do Elijah's actions in the presence of God show us? (**Elijah's depressed feelings are self-centered and run deep.**)

What was God doing by focusing Elijah's attention on himself? (**He was exposing the source of Elijah's real problem.**)

How does Elijah's repeated answer to God make it clear that he still had much to learn? (**He didn't change a word. The experience had not shaken him from his depressed self-centeredness.**)

Read verses 15 to 18

How does God address Elijah's needs in these verses? (**He shows Elijah that he [God] is in control. He offers Elijah a meaningful course of action. He reveals other leaders who will help fulfill God's purpose. He assures Elijah that his work has not been in vain, that 7,000 in Israel have remained faithful to God.**)

What is God aware of that Elijah is not thinking about? (**God is aware of the long-range plan and the unseen results of his plan so far.**)

How does God demonstrate his patience with his servant? (**He works with Elijah and reenlists him in his service.**)

What do God's commands to anoint other servants demonstrate to Elijah and us about God's control? (**He indicates that he has a long-range plan that will be carried out. He does not depend solely on us. We should depend entirely on him.**)

How might this question of who is in control cause Elijah to feel isolated, depressed, and anxious? (**When Elijah felt that he had to be in control, he was devastated when things seemed to get out of control. He left himself nowhere to turn.**)

Psalm 32

Read verses 1 to 2

How does David's experience add meaning to his expression of the blessing of forgiveness in these verses? (**David had committed two horrendous sins [adultery and murder] and personally experienced what it meant to have those sins forgiven, covered, and not counted against him by the Lord.**)

How does David appear in these verses to be longing for something he has lost? (**David had lived with sin and deceit, and one might sense a feeling of penitent regret [loss of self-sufficiency] as he recounts the blessings of forgiveness.**)

How does David describe forgiveness in a way that would comfort a person who is depressed and thinking about his own guilt? (**He shows that the Lord does the forgiving and his forgiveness is complete. The depressed person doesn't do anything to earn forgiveness. The Lord covers and no longer counts the sins.**)

Read verses 3 to 4

What are some of the typical signs of depression in these verses? (**David's mood was extremely low. His sleep patterns were affected ["day and night"]. He felt a heaviness on him and had no strength to respond.**)

What physical suffering does David describe? (**He wasted away. His strength was sapped. He groaned under his burden.**)

How does David describe his emotional suffering? (**He suffered in silence. He felt constantly oppressed. He sensed the hand of the Lord upon him.**)

How does David's physical and emotional suffering relate to his spiritual condition? (**David "kept silent" about his sin. He did not confess and seek forgiveness. This silent sinfulness caused him to fret and to feel God's disapproval and to fall into his physically and emotionally depressed state.**)

Why does this relationship between the physical, emotional, and spiritual exist? (**God made us human beings with body and soul inseparable in this life. When we experience problems, our whole being must deal with the results.**)

Why was David fertile ground for Satan when he was in this state? **(David had pushed God out of the picture.)**

Read verse 5

Why did David finally confess his sins (remember 2 Samuel 12:1-14)? **(The Prophet Nathan confronted him.)**

What does this teach us about the need for a Christian friend or counselor when one is in a state of depression? **(We may be beyond acknowledging our sin and guilt [as it may relate to our depression] unless someone confronts us with God's truth.)**

What were the benefits of confession? **(David broke his oppressive silence. The burden was exposed. God forgave his guilt.)**

Why is confession more than a psychological release? **(For complete relief, the person needs to learn of the Lord's forgiveness.)**

What is the most important part of a Christian's confession of sins? **(The Christian turns to the Lord for forgiveness.)**

Read verses 8 to 11

What indications does Scripture provide that David's suffering was over? **(David became active again, teaching others of God's counsel. He calls for trust and rejoicing. He turns attention to God instead of to himself.)**

What indications does the psalm provide that David truly believed and appreciated God's forgiveness? **(He witnesses to the Lord's unfailing love.)**

What did David's appreciation for God's forgiveness prompt him to do? **(David's appreciation prompted him to rejoice in the Lord and be glad.)**

How is David a model for us in our concern about others who might be depressed? **(David actively instructed and counseled others so that they, too, might know the Lord's unfailing love.)**

Philippians 1

Read verses 3 to 11

How does Paul demonstrate his love and concern for the Philippians? **(Paul longs for them, and he prays for them.)**

How does he show that he considers their concerns understandable? (**Paul has them "in [his] heart."**)

What do the Philippians appear to be overlooking in their concerns for Paul? (**They may be looking at his chains and overlooking God's grace at work among them.**)

How is Paul's concern for the Philippians an indication that Paul was not depressed in his difficult situation? (**Paul does not center his attention on himself, but on the Philippians and their needs.**)

Read verses 12 to 14

How is God's control evident in Paul's life? (**Paul sees his imprisonment as a means to fulfill God's will.**)

How was God's control able to do more than any human being could accomplish? (**God's control put Paul in a position to witness even to the palace guards, and to encourage others to speak the Word of God more courageously.**)

How did God keep his promise to make all things work out for the good of Paul and Christ's Church? (**God used Paul's imprisonment to advance the gospel.**)

Why would understanding this control of God prevent a person from falling into a depression that has spiritual roots? (**When we understand God's control in this way, we are far more ready to trust completely in him no matter what our human conditions are. We have no reason to be depressed when God is in control.**)

Read verses 18 to 26

What gave Paul the confidence that God would take care of him in his current situation? (**Paul was strengthened by the prayers of the Philippians and by the Spirit of Jesus Christ. And he rejoiced because even in his seemingly bad situation, Christ was being preached.**)

What was the extent of Paul's confidence? (**Paul was confident that even in his [Paul's] death, Christ would be exalted.**)

What was Paul's primary concern? (**Paul's primary concern was for the spiritual well-being of the Philippians.**)

What was the difference between St. Paul's desire to depart and be with the Lord and thoughts of suicide a depressed person might have? **(Paul was reflecting on the unparalleled blessings of heaven, but he was fully prepared and happy to continue the work that God gave him to do on earth. A suicide wants only to escape this life.)**

What showed that Paul was willing either to die or to live in contentment? **(Paul noted that "to live is Christ and to die is gain." He couldn't lose. He was "tuned in" to God.)**